MW01633730

# ACHIEVE SUCCESS WITH YOUR NEW TUTORING BUSINESS

A COMPLETE AND PRACTICAL BREAKDOWN FOR RUNNING A SUCCESSFUL TUTORING BUSINESS

ANDREW-JOHN PATERSON

# CONTENTS

Published in 2021 by miniteaching media Copyright © A-J Paterson 2021

Achieve Success with your New Home Tutoring Business

A-J Paterson 2021 © FIRST EDITION

miniteaching.com, contact hello@miniteaching.com

This is a work of creative nonfiction. Some parts have been fictionalised in varying degrees, for various purposes.

All rights reserved. No part of this book may be reproduced or modified in any form, including photocopying, recording, or by any information storage and transmission or retrieval system, without the permission of the copyright owner except for the use of quotations in a book review. Contact hello@miniteaching.com

No part of this book shall be by way of trade or otherwise, be lent, re-sold, hired out, in any form of binding or cover other than that in which it is published and without a similar condition including this condition being imposed on the subsequent purchaser.

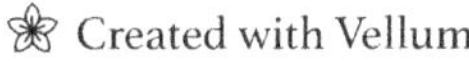 Created with Vellum

# ACKNOWLEDGMENTS

I would like to thank you for choosing my book to help guide you on your journey, into beginning a new life-changing tutoring business. You already may be a tutor or teacher currently working teaching a small number of students and looking to expand into a part-time or full-time business. This book will guide you in the right direction to establish a successful tutoring business with an excellent reputation. It has been written with much self-reflection from my own education and tutoring service practice over the past thirty years.

I thank my parents and family, especially my partner and children whom I love dearly, for their patience, support, and encouragement throughout my educational career.

I thank all the students I have ever taught and their achievements, fun, insights and humour that have made everyday teaching, so rewarding.

# ABOUT THE AUTHOR

Andrew resides in London, England, and worked as a teacher, Headteacher, School Education Consultant and current Principal of a tutoring service. He is the author of books and articles on school leadership and personal self-development. Andrew has taught in, and led, a number of Government and Private schools and holds a UK National Professional Qualification for Headteachers, Advanced Skills Teaching certification, a Bachelor of Education (Honours), a Post-Graduate Diploma in Counselling, and a Post-Graduate in Business Management.

With so many complicated and often confusing school curriculums, Andrew is driven to teach minimal, highly engaging and experiential lessons, resulting in his pupils' higher attainment and love for learning.

You can find out more about his educational service and the possibility of joining his educational service by visiting: miniteaching.com

facebook.com/Miniteaching-and-Alexandra-Park-Tutoring-101016735677830

instagram.com/miniteaching

# INTRODUCTION

**Why Tutoring?**

Tutoring is a rewarding and fulfilling occupation where you can make a positive difference to a young person's life. Many students are not a great match for the school system and need alternative, further encouragement, and guidance in their education. After all, we aren't all suited to certain educational systems in our society. We are neuro-diverse learners trying to fit in with regimented curriculums and teaching approaches.

Whether you work with children or adults, your teaching aims to inspire and empower them to love to learn through your specialty subject.

Unlike teachers who must try to reach many individual learning styles in a classroom, as a tutor, you get to teach… really teach, and make a targeted difference.

You'll prepare for exams, work with school curriculums and topics you student needs guidance with, and help them improve in a particular subject that they're struggling in.

There is a growing demand for tutors, with many students in our high-pressure, modern society:

- refusing to attend school
- with more parents and students applying for private and grammar schools
- many more students preparing for university amidst tough competition
- and so many students needing support with accessing a good education due to additional learning challenges and difficulties

The demand for excellent tutoring services is evident. According to The Sutton Trust (suttontrust.com), the private tuition market is a continuously growing market, revealing that:

- Across England and Wales, about 25% of state-educated 11–16-year-olds have ever received private tuition (rising to 42% in London).
- Across England and Wales, about 10% of state-educated 11–16-year-olds received private tuition in 2015 (rising to 18% in London).
- Over the last decade, the proportion of 11–16-year-olds who have ever received private tuition in England and Wales has risen from 18% to 25%.
- Calculations for this report suggest that the private tuition market for 5–18-year-olds in England, Wales and Scotland is worth between £1-2 billion per year.
- Privately educated students are about twice as likely to receive private tuition as state-educated students, according to multiple estimates.
- Poorer students are less likely to receive private tuition. Of those aged between 11-16, 17% of students who receive free school meals (FSM) have ever received private tuition, 26% of students who do not receive FSM.
- Nearly half (43%) of state schoolteachers have tutored outside of their main teaching role at some point during their lives.

- In London, of state-educated students aged between 11-16, over 150,000 (42%) have received private tuition at some point in their lives.

**By becoming a tutor, you open your life to:**

**1. Employment Flexibility**

Tutor as your own boss. There is no nine to five, it's flexible and convenient on your terms. Scheduling your workload gives you the opportunity to accommodate work around personal commitments, resulting in a better work-life balance.

You choose your days and how many hours you want to work, and even whether you work in person or online. It's likely that your local students will have school during the week so won't be able to see you until after 3pm or on weekends. There are chances to pick-up daytime ours tutoring students who don't attend school:

- those who are school refusers due to anxiety or other issues around school
- students with long-term illness
- home-schooled students whose parents need variety in their teaching
- overseas students in other time zones who you can teach online

**2. An increased income**

You may already be working as a teacher and want to earn some extra money on the side.

Maybe you have a completely different day job or a degree that you really feel the need to share your knowledge after all your hard study. As a student yourself, you can tutor those in younger year groups than you.

As a tutor, your skills and knowledge may be in high demand. English, languages, mathematics, physics, chemistry and biology are typically in popular. Computing and coding are also growing in popularity.

If you have competition within your subject area, you must build a great reputation by offers and a service that make you stand out from your competition within an excellent practice. This does not mean a lower price. A great reputation and great skills bring a higher price as will be discussed in Part 3 of this book.

### 3. Frequent Rewards

Every session you teach is bespoke and focused on the learning style and needs of one student. They'll learn far more in one session than possibly days of teaching in a large classroom. You can respond immediately to your student's learning and confidence needs, and break areas down as you encounter confusion or frustration. There's also immediate feedback through asking and answering questions. You'll be making a real difference in each of your students' lives.

You can be a role-model for your student and help them to grown in their academic ability and their confidence. By making your topic and the learning process engaging and exciting, they will learn to love learning. When you start to see your student achieve in their exams and schoolwork, it will give you a true sense of gratification and pride for your efforts and theirs.

### 4. Further Personal Learning

Teaching is a way of clarifying your own knowledge and keeping your excitement for learning fresh information on your subject of study. Those we teach, teach us. You'll build and reinforce your skills in delivery as a teacher as you're exposed to different learning styles. You'll gain new insights through your student's fresh insights. Your communication and leadership skills will improve and carry to other areas of your life. You will personally grow!

By practicing your knowledge, you become highly knowledgeable in the area you're tutoring in. You will have to ensure that you are always one step ahead of your student's learning and doing your own revision along the way.

Being a tutor is something that will always be in demand. The bonus is, if you love to teach, it will positively change your life for the better.

1

# PRIVATE TUITION IN THE UK

## Qualifications to Tutor

In May 2013, The Centre for Market Reform began the process of forming The Tutors Association to ensure minimum standards of education for private tutors, plus a code of ethics for which all members abide. It's proposed that Secondary tutors hold University degrees in their subject area and Primary tutors hold a general degree in any subject. Tutors should be significantly more qualified than the students they tutor.

https://thetutorsassociation.org.uk

Qualified teachers are often preferred by their parents for their Safeguarding knowledge and their professional registration with the DfE. If you intend to work as a tutor in a school or college, you'll require a Postgraduate Certificate of Education (PGCE).

If you work as a tutor in an independent school, an equivalent qualification from another country or a degree in a desired subject is often acceptable.

## DBS: Disclosure and Barring Service

Anyone in the UK who works with young or vulnerable people needs to undergo a Criminal Records Bureau (DBS) check. Although, private tutors are not required to apply for a DBS, it is still in your interests and your employers to at least apply for a basic check.

Umbrella companies, can help you attain one. Here is one example:

https://www.carecheck.co.uk/products/basic-dbs-checks/

## Types of Criminal Records Check

There are 3 types of criminal records check. The employer or organisation requesting the check should provide the applicant with more information about what level of check is required.

### STANDARD DBS CHECK

A Standard DBS check costs £26 (as of 2021) and details spent and unspent convictions, cautions, reprimands, and final warnings. It normally takes about 2 weeks for a standard check to process.

### ENHANCED DBS CHECK

Enhanced checks cost £44 (as of 2021) and include all details outlined in a standard check plus any additional information held locally by police forces that is considered relevant to your profession.

### ENHANCED DBS with list checks

An Enhanced DBS with list checks costs £44 (as of 2021) and include all details outlined in an enhanced check and a check through the appropriate DBS barred lists.

.  .  .

DBS CHECKS for volunteers are free of charge. This includes anyone who spends time helping people and isn't being paid or isn't only looking after a close relative.

An employer can only apply for a check if the job or role specifically requires one. Employers must tell the applicant for what purposes they are being checked.

DBS checks don't have an official expiry date. Any information included will be accurate at the time the check was carried out. It is up to an employer to decide if and when a new check is needed.

Applicants and employers can use the DBS update service to keep a certificate up to date or carry out checks on an existing certificate for a potential employee.

## Tutoring Fees

In the UK, tutors earn on average £20 to £80 per hour, based on their experience and qualifications. If you are educated to degree level, don't undersell yourself in comparison to your competition. It has an impact on your reputation and the reputation of other tutors in the industry; after all, you must prepare for lessons, give and mark homework, track your student's progress, and spend money on resources and travel.

## Working for Yourself or Working for an agency, or both!

As discussed, by becoming a tutor, you can decide your working hours, which is often the main draw for many. You will need to market yourself to build your clientele. An agency like ours (miniteaching.com) will do most of your promotion and marketing for you. Our reputation has built through word-of-mouth and testimonials which attracts clients. We collect payments from clients directly to ensure you are paid on time. However, with effort and patience, you can do the same.

There are pros and cons for working solo or as part of an agency, and these will be discussed throughout the book.

## Where and How to Tutor

When deciding whether to tutor in your own home, in your student's home, or online (or all three), you should always consider your expenses. You have to be prepared to live on little income while you build up your practice, and therefore your expenses become significant.

- Will the cost of your utilities increase because of your tuition business?
- Do the costs outweigh the profit?
- Do you need public liability or professional indemnity insurance?
- Are you permitted to run a small business from your rented property?
- How far can you travel to make your earnings worthwhile and what are your travel expenses and fares?
- What about clients who cancel last minute? Who will handle it?
- Are you willing to give up evenings and possibly weekends?

## Finding Students at the Start of the School Term

Tutoring has its peaks and troughs. Students and parents typically begin their search for a tutor at the beginning of the school year in September, and also in January, after exams, first reports and parent's evenings.

## The UK Education System: Primary and Secondary

The National Curriculum governs what school-aged children are taught and assessed on their academic ability. The National

Curriculum determines the subjects and levels students are taught through Key Stages (KS), throughout their schooling:

- EYFS – Nursery and Reception (age 3-4)
- KS1 (age 5-7)
- KS2 (age 8-11)
- KS3 (age 12-14),
- KS4 GCSE (age 14+),
- KS5 6th Form, A Levels (age 17-18+)

The International Baccalaureate (IB) is also a popular choice for approved study in the United Kingdom and is on offer in certain State and Independent schools.

From the five to sixteen, children who attend state schools are expected to learn under the National Curriculum.

The aim of The National Curriculum is to ensure all children are taught the same subjects at the same level and receive the same coursework.

Schools have some freedom how The National Curriculum is taught as long as Educational, and Teaching Standards are adhered to. In England, the curriculum is set by The Teaching Agency. In Scotland, Learning and Teaching Scotland (LTS) determines the Scottish Curriculum.

Independent schools can teach different approved Curriculums under OFSTED (England) Independent Inspections (or their equivalent body.) Education Scotland, Estyn Wales, Education and Training Inspectorate Northern Ireland, and The Department of Education Republic of Ireland, are the education inspectorates in these countries.

Ofsted is the England Office for Standards in Education, Children's Services and Skills. They inspect services providing education for learners of all ages. They also inspect and regulate services that care for children and young people.

They report independently and impartially about school performance to Parliament and the Department of Education.

## 11 Plus Examinations and SATs (Standard Assessment Tests)

For many independent and grammar schools, students sit the Eleven Plus examination in their final year of primary school in order to be selected by performance in their desired school. SATs tests are run in state and some independent schools to judge progress in learning; however, this does not preclude an academically poor pupil from attending a State-run secondary school, which all students in England are entitled to do.

Many parents seek tutors to help their child familiarise and be more confident under these testing conditions as they can be quite stressful, particularly if their child has language, cognitive, medical or behaviour needs as well.

# PRIVATE TUITION IN THE UNITED STATES OF AMERICA

## The Educational System

The K-12 system progresses from kindergarten to 12th grade. Children begin school around the age of five and continue through to the age of eighteen.

THERE ARE THREE STAGES:
Elementary School (Grades K to 5)
Middle School (Grades 6 to 8)
High School (Grades 9 to 12)

HERE YOU CAN ROUGHLY MATCH the equivalents between the key stages in the UK and the USA.

| UK YEAR | Age of student | US GRADE |
| --- | --- | --- |
| Nursery | 3–4 | Preschool |
| Reception | 4–5 | Preschool |
| Year 1 | 5–6 | Kindergarten |
| Year 2 | 6–7 | Grade 1 |
| Year 3 | 7–8 | Grade 2 |
| Year 4 | 8–9 | Grade 3 |
| Year 5 | 9–10 | Grade 4 |
| Year 6 | 10–11 | Grade 5 |
| Year 7 | 11–12 | Grade 6 |
| Year 8 | 12–13 | Grade 7 |
| Year 9 | 13–14 | Grade 8 |
| Year 10 | 14–15 | Grade 9 |
| Year 11 | 15–16 | Grade 10 |
| Year 12 | 16–17 | Grade 11 |
| Year 13 | 17–18 | Grade 12 |

*UK to US conversion*

In the United States, education is state and local government led. Every single state has a Department of Education and its own laws governing finance, recruiting staff, curriculum, and attendance. States decide whether education is compulsory, and to what age.

STANDARDISED TESTING in schools has become an issue, in that students sit around 112 standardised tests between kindergarten and 12th grade. In December 2015, President Obama signed the "Every Student Succeeds" Act, where every child in the US, regardless of race, income, background, the zip code, or where they live must be offered the same opportunities for education. This act replaced the "No Child Left Behind Act of 2002." The recommendations are for fewer tests of a higher quality.

INDIVIDUAL STATES MUST TEST students in reading and maths from Grades 3 to 8, and once during their high school years. Unlike **A Levels** in the UK or the International **Baccalaureate Diploma**, US students leave school with a collection of assessments that demonstrates their readiness for either college or work.

Some schools issue a high-school diploma on completing Grade 12, but it is not standardised and will vary between individual states.

. . .

AT THE END of high school, students receive a Grade Point Average (GPA), which can help determine their journey into work or college. The GPA is an average score taken from a student's high school career through tests: mid-term exams, final exams, essays, quizzes, homework assignments, classroom participation, group work, projects, and attendance. Students can also receive a class rank, where their GPA is levelled in comparison to all the other students within their grade.

## Standardised Testing

The US Federal Government has attempted to standardise the curriculum across US schools through the "**Common Core.**" The Common Core is a set of high-quality academic standards in mathematics and English language, and arts. It outlines what a student should know and practise, at the end of each grade.

MANY STATES HAVE ADOPTED the Common Core, with a few states having withdrawn from the Common Core and then developing their own sets of standards.

## SATs and ACTs

Many students opt to take either the SAT (Scholastic Aptitude Test) or ACT (American College Test), nationally recognised tests taken at high-school level. Highly ranked Universities require applicants to submit scores from either the SAT or the ACT. A high-test score is required for entry.

THESE EXAMS ARE VERY different to the UK and international tests. The tests are multiple-choice and cover four areas: English, maths, reading and science. There is also an optional writing test, which measures a student's skill in planning and writing an essay. Those outside of the US can also sit the ACT and the SAT to enter US Higher Education institutions.

## Advanced Placement

The Advanced Placement (AP) is a programme of learning and assessment for Higher Education Institutions to assess students for entry into College and University. It has been developed by the College Board, who also govern the SAT tests.

The AP is linked to the first year of College in the US, so students follow a subject they hope to continue studying at college level. The AP is thorough in comparison to the standard high-school courses and compares similarly with A Levels and the International Baccalaureate, the gold-standard qualification for university preparation.

While the AP is not necessary for entry into US Higher Education, students often take the programme to demonstrate a commitment to the subject they hope to study in the future.

# PART I

# BE AN OUTSTANDING TUTOR

1

## TUTORING IS TEACHING… AND COACHING

Do you consider teaching a calling rather than just a profession or job?

Does paperwork and assessment affect your love for teaching?

What makes education different to indoctrination and what do you personally do about it?

Should we waste time teaching students what they already know just because we haven't checked exactly what they do and don't know?

Have you noticed how controlling some schools really are and what affect this control has on a students' ability to learn and love learning?

Does a controlling approach affect a teacher's ability to inspire and encourage learning?

### The problem with Teaching and Schooling

Many people fail to understand the complexity of teaching and learning processes. They see teaching as a series of learnable activities and teachers as simply following textbooks to produce educated students. Everybody seems to regard education as a quick and easy 'fix.'

YOU'VE HEARD **the varying comments from the public:**

- "Teachers should be teaching these kids respect."
- "Teachers must focus on the three R's if they want to fix education."
- "Teachers shouldn't complain how difficult their job is when they get so many holidays."
- "Teachers don't teach right from wrong, that's why we have problems in our society."
- "Teachers teach because they can't get a job in what they trained in."

GENERAL CRITICS MUST UNDERSTAND that there is no 'fixing' in teaching, as no student is 'broken.'

EVERY YEAR there are new demands being introduced for teachers to adopt as a part of their teaching role, such as counselling, welfare, social and political change. You entered the profession to teach and inspire, and you now find your teaching time overwhelmed by extra roles, responsibilities, and an increasing amount of paperwork that distances you from focusing on your students' progress.

So, many professionals have attempted to re-engineer curriculums, timetables, the school day, manipulate subjects like English and Mathematics, and constrict the teaching practices that the teachers have used successfully in the past to deliver a checklist of teaching standards. Therefore schools, management and teachers are under constant scrutinisation from outside agencies such as OFSTED and their equivalent in the UK and Republic of Ireland, and School Inspectors in the US.

STANDARDISED CURRICULUMS AND TESTING, policies to hold every aspect of a school to account takes up teachers' time which is not what they originally signed up for. Teachers enter the profession to teach, yet with cuts in administration, much of the administration now falls upon a teacher's daily duties. This is on top of planning, student tracking, report writing, school meetings, parent meetings, and subject management demands.

WHEN THESE STRATEGIES fail to produce the results they want, policymakers and politicians, the media and then the public resort to blaming teachers and managers for not making adequate yearly progress in line with policymakers planning.

POLICYMAKERS ARE TYPICALLY OUT of touch with the realities of the classroom and the realities of the financial cutbacks that schools operate under.

SCHOOLS ARE NOT factories for learning; they are a safe place for nurturing student knowledge, interaction, and socialisation. Some say that technology will replace schools. Education cannot be replaced by technology anytime soon, as the social interaction and the flexibility for thinking is not yet ready. Currently, technology is a tool for enhancing learning, not a replacement for school.

·  ·  ·

***BEING** **an effective teacher is a very difficult job and does not garner the respect it deserves.***

Teachers teach, listen, discuss, create, nurture, counsel, study, adapt, role-model, simulate learning experiences, care, are passionate about learning, and put up with a lot of disrespect, not necessarily from their students, but from their own departments, some management, and the society around them. However, there are many, including parents and appreciative management, who praise, respect, and appreciate the patience and efforts that teachers put into their students.

A GREAT TEACHER plans and delivers engaging lessons and activities for learning; empathises with their students; differentiates a variety of classroom learning activities for individual students and those in small groups; works with children with extra educational needs; manages behaviour in a positive and constructive way; and cares deeply for the progress of their students.

THE ODDS of teaching as the only part of their job, is unusual. Teaching is only 50 to 70% of a typical teacher role. Unfortunately, stress comes from the high number of students in the classroom and the paperwork that accompanies both their class and the wider school. Paperwork to be put before administrators on a regular basis, which rarely benefits the teacher in their art of teaching.

*Tutoring, on the other hand...*

Tutors have all the odds stacked in their favour. A tutor is chosen to help a child progress. There are no politics and paperwork to govern how it must be done. A tutor can trust their abilities as a professional to do what they consider right to improve their student's performance. A teacher has learned an art, a craft they have honed over the years to create learning in their classroom, and they can now return to this through tutoring.

IF TUTORS WANT their students to love learning, they can offer the personal approach and talents that those teachers stuck in paper-driven schools are unable to.

2

# LEARNING IS AN EMOTIONAL JOURNEY

Learning is an intellectual and emotional experience. Learners can experience anxiety and fear when presented with new challenges in their education. Fear or hesitance in the face of the unfamiliar is a universal experience for us all. We all feel discomfort or even paralysis in the face of the unknown. It is our natural protective response of "fight or flight" instinct we have inherited from centuries of human evolution.

Sometimes we can reframe this fear into excitement as the same adrenaline is released for both feelings.

Tutors use their sense of what is too challenging and what is just enough challenge by reading the expressions and reactions of their students or by asking for their direct feedback. Some students will just straight-up tell you that a challenge is too difficult.

However, there is also the need to develop a student's resilience. This takes gentle introduction, rather than the overwhelm of too much information we think they need to know or should know. You are a guide for your student, showing them the way to take the next step. You are not a taskmaster.

Often a student experiences many emotions, and they vary from lesson to lesson. Don't blame yourself if your student is feeling tired or overwhelmed. Work with what they have to offer in the moment. We do our best with the state that we are feeling in the moment.

**HERE ARE some ways to teach them directly or indirectly how to get them out of this state:**

- Break things down into easier chunks.
- Distract them with something energising and fun, such as a game or a physical movement activity.
- Play to their interests and experiences.
- Ask them to have a go at teaching something to you.
- Turn the concept you are teaching into a creative genre, such as a drawing, mindmap, list of points or mini booklet or comic.
- Dramatize a concept into a mini performance.
- Use design software and create a presentation, animation, or cartoon to illustrate the learning.

***WHEN THE WIND** **of emotion blows your session in a stormy direction, you need to change tact.***

LIKEWISE, you don't want to be experiencing the doldrums. The one emotion we don't want learners to feel too often is **"This is boring."**

Boredom signals a lack of effective engagement. An engaged student is curious, committed, alert, and demonstrates a sense of purpose.

An unengaged student is defeatist in their talk and actions. Indifference leaves a student immobile and non-receptive.

Plan your lessons considering the emotional variety of your student and include in your plan a number of engagement activities and contingencies.

CONSIDER the emotional responses you want your student to have in your planned activities and design them into your lesson plans. Use simulations and models wherever possible to get your student interacting with their learning.

Recently, I have found Virtual Reality amazing for teaching subjects as complex as Shakespearian language can be. There are loads of VR videos now available on YouTube. This is an example of using new technology as a tool for learning.

EMOTIONAL CHALLENGE STRETCHES the learner beyond what they believe they can do and encourages a deeper understanding for what they can achieve.

Gently persuade your student out of their comfort zone by having a go of a new practise without the fear of failure.

WE ALL MUST STRETCH a little to grow intellectually and emotionally. A good teacher will raise education from its dead state on a page and make it come alive though simulated action.

## Engaging Positive Emotions

Give your students a lesson they will not forget! Challenge them to examine, explore, and experiment rather than drag up facts that any google search can do.

.   .   .

CREATIVE TEACHERS PLAN lessons that generate a positive emotional response. Emotion enhances learning and makes facts memorable because we are sensory in our learning. We learn through our eyes, ears and by moving our bodies.

WHEN EMOTIONS ARE ENGAGED, the tutor can step aside and guide, and their student can make rapid gains in learning. This is how you move your student from knowledge to application. Many children and teens can memorise facts, but by vocalising them, and acting them out through simulations, they develop their understanding in a deep dive into a concept.

**Mastery comes from independently applying learning successfully.** Shorten the route by taking any opportunity to simulate learning. It gives your student the chance to test it out and absorb a concept.

3

# IMPROVING TEACHING AND LEARNING

**Engagement**

Get in the habit of beginning your teaching by stirring imagination and excitement for a new concept. A real-life model or demonstration shortcuts a whole lot of wasted learning time. You want this activity to be something that evokes their curiosity and sense of mystery. You need to call your student to action.

Learning is mostly fun. Sometimes it is hard work, but eventually it should always return to a sense of fun and reward. You don't want a reluctant, uninspired student on your hands as a result of your lack of inspiration.

Tell stories about the fun you experienced when you first learnt a concept that you now teach. Tell a story about some great person who overcame adversity to discover the concept.

Talk about the fun of discovery, the satisfaction of working hard and learning to do something well. Passionately talk about it often. Share your enthusiasm and mean it. Not as a preacher or speech maker, but as an excited teacher. Enthusiasm is contagious. So too is a lack of enthusiasm, which is the source of many people's tales of being bored at school.

Once you have roused students' curiosity, spur their imaginations and creativity with an inspiring activity. Make a plant cell out of card, stand up and recite a poem, or play a beat to emphasise iambic pentameter. Write a line each of a partnered creative story and model how to construct a sentence as you do so. Play a grammar game by reading a sentence and having your student hold up cards with the correct punctuation. Use your imagination and step out from the ordinary, and you will be an extraordinary tutor.

**Listen out for obstacles to your students learning**

- Listen when a student is disappointed or discouraged. Let them discuss how they feel about the things that discourage them. Help them change the feeling, by guiding them to the feelings that are in their control.
- Ask, "What can we do right now to change this feeling?" Teach them that they have control over their feelings by thinking of what can be done to pull them out. Sometimes some jumping jacks and movement can help energise and distract your student and bring their attention back to what you are teaching.
- Model how you manage mistakes when you make them. Deliberately make an error in your maths or writing and show them how you self-correct. Then ask them what they could do to self-correct and get them to practise it.
- Read about people who have overcome failure and eventually achieved success: Sports stars such as Serena Williams and engineers like Elon Musk have expressed plenty of moments of failure and how they pulled things together. There are plenty of examples of inventors who have faced many failures on their route to discovery. Balance genders, cultural backgrounds, and occupations within your stories.
- Encourage your student to continue to "try" with your

help and guidance. Move them to practising a sum or concept independently by scaffolding the task.

## Student Centred Approach

Home tuition requires a more student-centred approach than in a classroom.

Philosopher Carl Rogers espoused that students do not learn effectively through direct teaching and only they themselves can facilitate their learning.

The tutor is the guide as their knowledge is beyond their student, helping that student grasp new concepts by drawing upon their experiences and developing their understanding of new concepts through practise, simulations, and demonstrations. Admitting that you are not sure of an answer to a question, and letting your student know that you'll need to find out, will demonstrate that we all have to research.

## Developing Student Learning

The tutor must clearly know the student's starting point to ascertain where the student needs to improve. Strengths and weaknesses help reveal the strategies needed to improve their understanding and performance. By breaking knowledge into steps and using goal-setting strategies in the form of small, manageable tasks and actions, a student consequently feels they are in control and responsible for their own learning which increases motivation.

This is where a knowledge of past reports, where the student stands against the objectives of the subject curriculum, and summative and formative assessment is important. Run mini summary tests at the end of each unit of learning you teach to check your student's understanding. It doesn't necessarily need to be formal. It may be a student presentation, discussion, mini booklet of facts or creative writing. Use these summary checks to inform your next steps in planning.

. . .

Students need **guidance and coaching by:**

- Thinking together with the teacher
- Expressing ideas with their teacher's support and encouragement
- Learning to question things and finding their own answers to their questions, through teacher coaching
- Learning how to sort things out and organise ideas with their teacher providing models.

## Planning and Tracking Progress

To track your students starting point, and their progress from that point with you as their tutor, use the specific criteria of the curriculum the student is currently studying at school or the curriculum they are aiming for in their desired school. Don't be afraid to drop back a year or more for certain skills or prior knowledge that your student doesn't yet have. We must get the foundations of knowledge and skills in place before we can advance a student who is behind their peer age group.

It is absolutely vital that you follow the curriculum and methods of the school curriculum from where they attend, otherwise your student will become confused by conflicting methods and knowledge. Many schools complain that tutors are teaching their students the wrong information or strategies. Align yourself with the school, or the school that the student is aiming to attend.

All approved curriculums and examinations from examination boards are available online for free, including SATs and 11+ examinations for many schools. Most schools publish their study curriculums on their website for transparency to parents and local officials. If they haven't, a request directly to the school should get you the information you require to tutor effectively.

Alternatively, many education subscription services, such as Twinkl.com and TES.com have dozens of curriculums, resources and tracking sheets to help you deliver a consistent and clear curriculum. You do not have to reinvent the wheel.

In the UK, use the National Curriculum, SATs questions, 11+ questions, or specific examination board such as OCR, AQA, Edexcel etc. that the student is studying or aiming to study.

## An Excellent Lesson

An excellent lesson should consider and follow the process of the following key moments:

1. Knowing your student's prior Knowledge, skills and understanding
2. Linking the learning in the previous session through quick revision
3. Having one (not many!) clear Learning Intention/objective
4. Delivering the Key Vocabulary, the student must know for the topic
5. Planning and asking Key questions that will draw out your student's understanding.
6. Success criteria to know what constitutes the child's successful understanding and application of the topic or concept you have taught.
7. An Introduction where you provide a model of the outcome and what a successful outcome will look like. A demonstrated simulation of what you are teaching. The student should not have to read your mind for what you deem to be successful.
8. The main activities and experiences in your lesson must begin with the student's prior knowledge and introduce the challenge/slight stretch of new knowledge. This differentiation and introduction of the next steps are vital to progress.
9. Mini-assessments or knowledge checks between activities to make sure your student is on track.

10. A Conclusion/Plenary which summarises the learning and checks the overall learning.
11. Throughout the lesson, planned cross-curricular links and links with the student's experiences and interests should be evident.
12. An evaluation of what they now know whether knowledge needs to be revisited, and next steps in their learning.

QUESTIONS TO ASK **yourself when planning an excellent tutoring session:**

1. Does my student already know this, or do I need to confirm their knowledge?
2. What do we need to recap about the last session to provide continuity with this session?
3. What is the one most important thing I want my student to learn from this session?
4. What key vocabulary must they know for this topic?
5. What key questions can I ask to check their understanding?
6. How will I know they have grasped this topic/concept? What will I use as a written, practical, or verbal assessment?
7. What model can I use to engage their interest right from the start?
8. What activity can I provide that will build from what they know to a stretch in their understanding?
9. What are some quick, fun checks of their understanding so far in this lesson?
10. What activity or question can I ask to draw out a summary of the lesson to check their overall performance? You want this reflection to be in the student's own words.

11. How can I link my lesson to a past lesson or an interest they have expressed?

12. How did the lesson go in terms of the feedback I received from the student? What do I need to review to make it more successful in the future? What worked well that I can use again?

TUTORS MUST RESPOND to each student's emerging needs and interests, guiding their development through warm and encouraging interaction.

## Make your activities relevant, Challenging and Fun

Our aim is to move the student into a flow of learning.

Flow is the state of being completely involved in an activity for its own sake and using your student's skills to the utmost through challenge, where distractions don't even enter their thoughts.

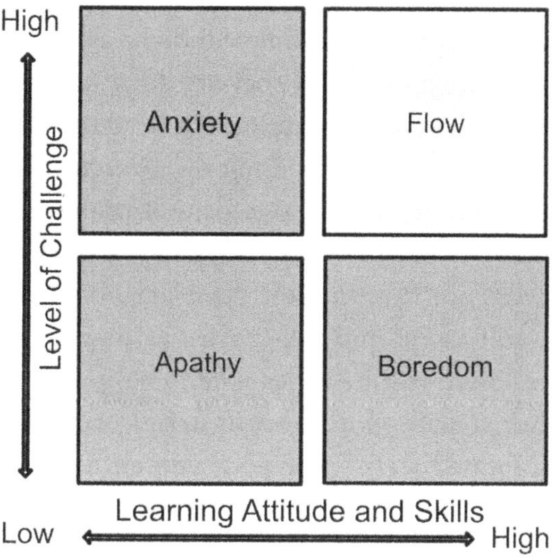


*Flow of Learning*

## SUMMARY of the Essential Elements you should consider for an Excellent Lesson

1. Tasks are appropriately challenging.
2. Teacher Input is balanced with the student's input. The session is structured for students to work collaboratively with their tutor or other tutees. Try to keep your teacher talk below 60% and prompt you student to respond most of the time. If you are speaking 80 to 100% of the time, this is a sign that you are not listening to, or allowing, your student's response.
3. Tutoring has necessary elements to deliver, which can be broken down into: attitudes, skills, concepts and knowledge, comprehension and understanding, and

habits. These can all be delivered through good tutor simplification and modelling.

4. Goals are clear and worthwhile. Students are clear on what they're doing and why they are doing it. Progress is reflected when a student can explain what they are doing and why they are doing it in their own words.

5. Feedback is immediate in the form of prompts, "What punctuation should we put at the end of this command?" etc. We want to create learners who can learn to self-assess and self-correct as they are working. However, there will be times when you ignore errors for higher goals; you don't want to be correcting spelling immediately when your student is in the flow of creative writing. Save the spelling check until the end.

6. Teaching is about moving students toward becoming self-motivated learners. Intrinsic motivation is when your student wants to learn through inner interest and enjoyment, not through Extrinsic motivation where they are being forced to learn.

7. We want your student to develop competence in key skills and strategies that raise their success rate, which leads to better confidence and self-esteem.

8. Make new information relevant by starting with a relatable experience and then stretch them beyond what they know. Use what they read, watch on TV, and play with for relatable experiences.

9. Give choice to avoid having to do something just one-way. They have to personally decide what technique works best for them.

10. Make it fun and use humour (not sarcasm) at their level. Play with words and language.

11. Stir Imagination and curiosity. Themes such as fantasy, superpowers, magic, time travel, space travel and Science-Fiction can really stir a student's enthusiasm. Life is

exciting when we see the possibilities for improving ourselves, our experiences, and the world.

12. Engagement should be viewed as a hook to catch your student's interest.

## Start all sessions with introductory hooks

Engage your students from the outset of your lesson with anything that piques their interest, establishes relevance, or inspires curiosity in your subject, for example:

- A brainteaser or challenge question
- An historical example
- A video or audio clip
- A philosophical question
- A mystery
- A recent discovery
- A problem to solve
- A mission
- An invention
- A mysterious object
- A new technology – design software, a robot, virtual reality

## Engaging Broad Thinking when Problem-Solving

**Breaking Assumptions:** We all make assumptions about our world and how it operates without questioning things. List assumptions about a concept or piece of knowledge you are looking at. Then ask under what conditions these assumptions are not true. This is a great way to get perspective on a character in a story or an historic figure who is a product of the context of their times. How would they act or behave in modern times?

**Brainstorming:** Define the problem clearly and set the criteria to be met. Keep the session focused on the problem. Rank and prioritise the most important and relevant points.

**Concept or Mind Mapping:** Focus on a question specifying the problem the map should resolve and write it in the centre of the page/whiteboard. List the key concepts that link to the problem. Look for cross-links between concepts, adding linking words to the lines between the concepts.

**Fishbone:** On a large sheet of paper or whiteboard, draw a long arrow across the middle of the page pointing to the right, to form the backbone of the "fish." Label the head of the arrow with the issue. Draw "bones" from this "fish" at 45 degrees, and label each with every cause of the problem that you think of. Redraw the fishbone so that the most important points are near the head.

**Kipling Questions:** Simply ask Who? What? When? Where? Why? and How? when problem-solving or decision-making.

**Reverse Brainstorming:** Instead of looking for solutions, ask "How could I cause this problem?" or "How could I make things worse?" Then find opposites to the worse case scenarios to find your solutions.

**SCAMPER:** Scamper is a check list that creates a new way to think about a seemingly difficult problem.

- **Substitute:** What can you substitute/replace?
- **Combine:** What can you combine or bring together somehow?
- **Adapt:** What can you adapt as a solution?
- **Magnify:** What strength can you focus on?
- **Put to other uses:** How can you put the thing to different or other uses?
- **Eliminate:** What can you eliminate?
- **Rearrange:** What can be rearranged in some way?

**Post-it Notes:** Use post-it notes to collect ideas in any order in a brainstorm. Once they are gathered together, sort them into some kind of order. This is very useful for composing an essay, report, or answer to a question.

**Storyboarding:** Like post-it notes, story boards can help order planning and ideas, sorting and prioritising in a linear sequence with a beginning and an end. Divide an A4 or Letter sized sheet of paper into 6 panels with a pen/pencil. Storyboard out your ideas like in a comic strip or movie, with drawings and captions.

**Reversal:** The reversal method takes a situation and tips it upside down, inside out, or back-to-front. Any situation can be "reversed," and be looked at in a new way. If you can't empathise with a villain in a story, look for ways where you can. Try completing a sum in reverse.

**Constraints:** Constraining the boundaries making it easier for your student to focus. Often, tasks are too overwhelming and are difficult to start.

- Write an 8-word sentence, a 20-word sentence, a 4-word sentence, a 4-word rhyming couplet etc.
- Write down three questions or points that summarise the session
- Write down 3 things you already know about this

**Ask good questions: good questions should be:**
Open-ended to avoid "yes/no" answers

Differentiated to offer a graduated increase in depth and complexity

Fair because you want to hear students' thoughts and opinions about what they know, not what they don't. Don't play mind-reading, "Guess what's in my head" games.

**SWOT analysis:** This technique is often used in business to assess the market and competition. Take a sheet of paper and draw 4 quadrants/squares.

In each quadrant write one of the following as a header per quadrant: Strengths, Weaknesses, Opportunities and Threats. It is a great technique for clarifying a character's motivation when character profiling in Literature. What are Lady Macbeth's: strengths? weaknesses? opportunities? threats?

4

# CONFIDENCE BUILDING

## State and Skill

Confidence is both a state of mind and a skill learned to maintain that state of mind that can be practiced. Everybody has doubts, and those who manage them quickly have developed the understanding that they alone are in control of their attitude. If a student is reliant on external praise and encouragement for their confidence, they hand over their confidence to outside forces.

If a student in control of their learning, is more confident in their ability to succeed in their learning. Familiarity, consistency and repetition of knowledge and skills can reassure a student that they are progressing along the right path. No student can succeed when constantly delivered new concepts beyond their current experience. Tutors know the students prior learning and build upon it.

## Positive, Appropriate and Specific Praise

Use positive language as much as possible, even when correcting a student's errors, and be specific about how the student is improving. Even when we make mistakes, we have opportunities to improve.

Reframe 'mistakes' into something encouraging. If you feel you must criticise, give constructive, workable, solution-focused criticism that is not a personal criticism of the student. You want your student to achieve, not leave a session feeling 'hopeless.' You can distance a criticism by putting it into the third person and using a character from a story or a well-known figure as the focus and then discuss how they turned a problem around. On the other hand, do not flatter and give empty, unspecific praise. We all want to say, "You're amazing/incredible/perfect!" but for what? You must be realistic and honest in your praise. You are genuinely trying to help your student to improve, not buttering them up so that they, or their parent/s, will like you.

## Replacing Limiting Beliefs

Avoid words such as 'can't', 'don't', 'won't', 'shouldn't' and 'never.' It won't motivate them to do better or lift their efforts, they will just hear the negativity of the word and feel that they've been scolded. Students are vulnerable and it's your responsibility to be the role-model, not the critic. Great tutors break learning down into small, manageable chunks and use demonstrations and different approaches to explain the details of their topic. Find out what your student doesn't understand and give a clear, concise explanation of the practice. Modern teachers are taught that if a child isn't learning, it's the teacher's responsibility to deliver in a way that is conducive to their student's understanding.

## Personality and Self Expression

Your student is unique and needs to feel safe to express their opinion at any time. An expression of opinion is often the way that people use to question and understand. It's the sign of a deep thinker. Tutoring is not being the teacher in front of a classroom of 30 students where some order must be maintained, it is the opportunity for deep learning and all questions to be pondered and answered. You student's opinions are as valid as your own. It is time to explore what works best as an answer or solution. Self-expression and encouraging a student's personality, is building upon their natural strengths.

## STRATEGIES FOR GETTING STUDENTS TO ASK THEIR QUESTIONS

1. From the first day of tutoring, encourage your student to ask questions.
2. Be prepared that in the beginning, students will ask simplistic questions. You can teach them to ask higher order thinking questions by asking open-ended questions that don't have a simple factual answer, age-appropriate questions, of course.
3. Don't judge a student's questions but help them form a better question.
4. Before beginning a unit, conduct a brainstorming session in which you encourage your student to formulate questions they would like to find answers to about the topic.
5. Model question-asking throughout a unit of learning. Ensure these questions don't have a simple recall answer.

Students grow in confidence when they feel that there is shared mutual respect, just as we do as adults. The safety a student feels to ask any question is a sign that you have gained their trust.

5

# CHALLENGING BEHAVIOUR

Y ou are likely to come across students who just don't engage with you or your subject. This is often expressed as boredom or even conflict.

Some behaviours are disruptive and become a problem when no progress is made in resolving them. Behaviour is an issue in many schools and is influenced by many factors, from upbringing, habits, psychological difficulties, and neurodiversity.

## Managing inappropriate and disruptive behaviour

Focus on delivering a great lesson that fits with your student's interests. If a student can't relate, then they will disengage. This may take extra exploration and preparation but remember that you are typically tutoring in times when your student is used to relaxing. They have usually just attended school and are likely to be tired, or it's the weekend.

Use what you have control over, such as improving your communication and delivery. Try different approaches and reflect on what's working and what is not.

Be honest, ask your student what it is about the lessons that they don't find interesting. This is the most direct way of uncovering how you can improve your delivery or whether tutoring is just not suitable for the student.

Make sure you have a system in place for tracking your student's progress and achievements. If a student can see small improvements in their learning, they will want to continue improving and learning. Highlight their progress to them and their parent/s.

Get the parent/s or guardian on-side with praising your student, so that their progress is recognised in a united way. Don't be afraid to give stickers, certificates, books, or minor prizes, even for students in their teens. However, first check with their parents that this is okay. Don't reward with sweets or other unhealthy items. Stationary, such as pens, erasers and sharpeners are always popular.

## 10 Behaviour Strategies for One-to-One and Group Sessions

1. As the teacher, and adult, you are "in charge". You make the rules and decisions, but you need to ensure the behaviour of your student is not a result of your own ill-preparedness or negative reactions. Students should believe that you are one step ahead of them and that you are there to support them with no judgement.

2. Students need to know what is expected of them through a set of rules which make desired behaviours clear and positive. The rules should tell the students what to do, rather than what not to do.

3. Reward the right behaviours immediately, in disproportion to the inappropriate behaviours. Give rewards for appropriate behaviours. Praise is the best reward in most situations, highlighting exactly what you admire or appreciate.

4. Always capture a student's full attention before addressing behaviour. In a group, everyone must be looking at you and not disengaged. Be totally clear in your instructions

and expectations. If you need to know if they have got it, ask them to tell you what behaviour is required right now to learn.

5. Know that low-level misbehaviour escalates if not dealt with quickly and consistently. What we ignore or encourage by giving attention to, grows. Rather than humiliating a student in front of their peers, find a calm and quiet space to let the student know that you see exactly what they're doing, and the consequence that follows. Remain calm, don't even sound slightly annoyed, and use eye contact.

6. Avoid confrontation at all costs. Never corner anyone as their response will be an instinctual "fight or flight," from a feeling of threat. Discuss making the right choice as consequences come from wrong choices.

7. Never start teaching until your student/all students are ready. You'll be wasting all your session time and lesson planning if your student/s aren't engaged. You need to get them in the right state of mind for learning, which means you may have to address their current state first. If they are tired, energise them, if they are in a bad mood, treat them to something they enjoy for a few minutes. Sometimes outside distraction is required to draw a student out from an internal bad mood or lack of confidence.

8. Always end your session on a positive note about their achievement and have a fun activity prepared. Psychologically, we tend to remember the first and last experiences of an activity, known as primacy and recency. Make sure these moments are memorable.

9. Always use positive language. Instead of "Stop talking", say "Time to listen." Our brains cancel out negative commands, such as "Don't do that!" and interpret "Do that!" instead; "Don't eat that yummy, chocolate chip cookie in front of you!" Use embedded commands where the choices lead to your desired outcome, such as

"either/or" – "You can either work quietly by yourself or quietly in a group." Use "when/then" to promote the positive rewards of completing a task, "When you have finished your maths, then we can play a fun maths game."

10. Use positive, open body language. No finger pointing, nor physically looking down in an intimidating way. Get eye contact first before you instruct. Use your voice to great effect as well. Rather than shouting, use a clear but calm voice, say their name, and utilise pauses to gain attention; "Amira... please focus on your work. If you can't complete it now... you'll finish it as extra homework."

**Importantly**

Smile often and be of good humour and cheer. Respect from others comes from respecting others, no matter what their age.

**Teach Resilience**

Use the 3M's: Milestone, Mission, and Method to feedback to students how they are progressing, and how they can improve.

- **Milestone: Where am I?**

"Here's where you are right now. The introduction to your story was very good.

- **Mission: Where am I going?**

"To improve your introduction so that you improve a level higher, you just need to add a few more techniques."

- **Method: How do I get there?**

"If you begin your story with an attention grabbing "hook" and follow with different sentence starts, you will reflect a better understanding of the importance of language to hold your reader's attention."

By using a constructive feedback method, your student will have an opportunity to see that they are on the right path and that improving their method is not beyond their ability.

# 6

# ADDITIONAL EDUCATIONAL NEEDS OR NEURODIVERSITY

It is inevitable that you will tutor students with additional learning needs as tutors are sought out by parents to support their child's extra challenges in learning. Parents will be seeking a way to help their child progress at school, lessen the gap in their learning and keep up with their peers. However, we must inform parents that we as tutors teach to their child's starting point and build upon it, whether it be, below or above their peers.

Confidence typically presents as a factor; any child who struggles, naturally doesn't feel good about themselves. Tutors typically work with students who experience slower processing, dyslexia, dyspraxia and dyscalculia, Autistic Spectrum Disorder and Attention Deficit Hyperactivity Disorder, to name just a few known areas of neurodiversity.

You must be mindful of the extent of the student's need and ensure that the parent/guardian is present to provide support. You may be tasked to teach functional skills curriculums for Maths and English, organisation and prioritisation, and socialisation skills. Your focus may be on engaging the student's attention and concentration for extended periods of time.

I am no expert when it comes to teaching children with Special

Educational Needs; however, in my career as a teacher, I have worked with many children with a variety of neurodiverse needs that affects their learning or physical capabilities. Teaching students with additional educational needs is an extremely rewarding, sometimes challenging, and wholly worthwhile practice.

First and foremost, you must recognise that each student has their own starting point, and you must ascertain exactly where that starting point is in every topic you teach.

The best way to help someone with SEN is to follow the education plan already drawn up by the school or educational needs specialist, as they will have specific targets and next steps for the student to attain. The parents will most likely have confidential reports on their child's educational difficulties which you must view.

If you accept a child with additional needs that significantly affects their learning, be as fully informed as possible. I always insist that I know exactly what the difficulties are and how they affect their learning, communication, behaviour, and esteem. You do not want the parents to hold back information about any aspect of their child that could affect the tutoring session.

* PLEASE NOTE, that you should never hold on to any student's report, for confidentiality, safeguarding and data protection reasons. Ask the parent to read and discuss any relevant documentation with you and take your own notes. Do not record full names or any other information that identifies the student or parents. Any information you do record must be locked away from possible public discovery and viewing.

IF YOU ARE NOT SEN trained, make it clear to parents that you aren't, and that you can't offer advice beyond academic teaching and progress.

Don't assess, offer advice, nor suggest approaches or schools in relation to your student's needs. You can suggest referrals to expert specialists for further advice if you know of them.

THE GOLDEN RULE of tutoring is,
*"Never make promises you can't meet and complete."*

IF YOU ARE a SEN specialist in one area of speciality, such as dyslexia, do not represent yourself in another area where you aren't qualified. SEN teachers must stick to the area they are qualified for, and further train in other areas if they wish to branch out.

**WHEN WORKING with students with additional needs consider applying the following advice where appropriate:**

- Don't fear special needs. It may be a new experience for you, but for your student, it's their everyday life. Act normally, be relaxed, calm, friendly, and understanding. Their needs are natural and need to be treated as such. Your student wants to be seen as a person, while having their limits and challenges respected.
- Assume the best of your student and that they mean well. They are most likely doing the best they can right now.
- Show adult patience and understanding if they struggle, as they may not yet be capable of everything their peers can manage.
- Give them extra time to follow directions and make transitions. Many tasks and activities can seem difficult or uncomfortable, and they may have trouble organising and prioritising.
- Don't mistake disobeying your direction for misbehaviour, they may simply need help.
- Use pre-drawn visual pictures to show the order of

activities you are going to be doing and the transitions in-between. There are plenty of visual timetable cards available online.

- Don't assume that someone with a physical or developmental disability is intellectually inferior. Treat them in an age-appropriate way.
- Allow extra time to respond to a question before jumping in and helping, and always ask before assisting, "Do you want me to help you answer this?" "Do you want me to help you move this?"

ABILITIES VARY day to day because of stress, tiredness, and medication. Expect each session to be potentially different. Make an agreement with the student's parent/guardian that they will inform you of their child's state before the session.

Your student may be insecure about their needs. Talk about it calmly and casually, without making a fuss. They need to sense that you care, and their needs are not a burden to you.

If you aren't sure about the source of their lack of response or their display of frustration, ask,

- "Do you need help with your book?"
- "Is the noise bothering you?"

Encourage independence and decision-making. Don't treat your student as helpless and jump in. This deprives them of exercising independence and resilience.

IF YOU MUST HALT a behaviour or refuse a request, say exactly why,

"I know you want to play with your phone. Unfortunately, we must keep moving so that we can finish learning our 3 times tables. We don't have time to stop for another 10 minutes."

Keep your voice positive but firm.

PEOPLE COMMUNICATE DIFFERENTLY, but that doesn't make their communication less than anyone else. You certainly shouldn't laugh or make fun of what they say.

Don't have expectations about how they should act. Be open-minded and get to know them as an individual.

MANY STUDENTS SIT within the wide range of ASD (autism spectrum disorder), this includes Asperger's Syndrome, considered a form of Autism. Here are some guidelines to help you tutor students diagnosed as living with Autism:

Body language is complicated, and people are diverse, look for clues in your environment if your student begins to act unpredictably.

Be polite and respectful and ask when you are not sure of their feelings or behaviour, rather than getting frustrated or confused.

- "I noticed you've been fidgeting a lot while we're talking. Is something the matter, or does this help you concentrate?"
- "Are you feeling sad, or are you thinking?"

MANY PEOPLE with autism relax their facial features when their mind is busy. This may include a faraway gaze, a slightly open mouth, and a lack of expression.

Some people's facial expressions don't reflect how they are truly feeling inside. A student may never smile but is happy.

Lining up objects is an activity some people with autism undertake when they are lost in thought.

If they are staring into space, they are likely deep in thought.

They can still hear you and you can regain their attention if you want them to listen.

Expect them not to make eye contact which can be distracting or painful for autistic people. Their eyes may be focused on anything else but you, however they are likely listening to what you are saying.

Quirky mannerisms and behaviours are symptoms and have a meaning behind them. Stimming is a **repetitive, unusual movement or noise** that often helps some autistic children and teenagers manage emotions or cope with overwhelming situations.

If an autistic person is stimming while talking to you, assume that it enhances rather than detracts from their focus. It is a form of self-regulation.

Autistic people may suppress stims out of fear of criticism when around someone they don't know or trust. If a person with autism stims openly around you, this means that they probably trust and feel safe around you.

Stimming has many meanings, depending on the situation. They may be an expression of emotion, a way to reduce stress or overload, a focusing aid, or something else.

- Facial expressions: Stimming while smiling usually means something different from stimming while frowning.
- Words and sounds: What they say, or the sounds they make can give clues towards their feelings.
- Context: Waving or flapping when shown something interesting may reflect excitement. However, the very same actions may be an expression of frustration or worry in a task that is too difficult.

SOMETIMES STIMMING HAS no emotional meaning at all.

LOOKING AWAY CAN BE a sign of thinking or being overwhelmed, not necessarily displeasure or fear about you. When sensory inputs are too much, or you are too physically close, an autistic person may look away.

They might also look away when asked a question because they are thinking. Wait quietly while they process and come up with an answer.

Looking away can be a sign of unhappiness. If you ask, "Are you ready to start work?" and they look away, they may be feeling unhappy about having the session because there is something else, they are preoccupied with.

Some people with autism will make faces that seem angry or peculiar. This freedom of expression often means that they are comfortable enough around you to not hold back on their natural behaviours, which is a good sign.

People with autism often experience anxiety and sensory issues that cause discomfort or pain.

Anxiety can lead to a meltdown or shutdown, and it is best that you notify the parent/guardian if you sense a stressed change in their behaviour.

Never use word or physical force to make a person with autism behave or conform. You may trigger a "fight or flight" response.

WHEN WORKING WITH SEN, never continue in a situation where you feel out of your depth supporting students beyond your academic teaching and coaching ability.

We cannot be experts in what we don't understand.

It is not a failure on your part; some students we encounter have been through a series of tutors as parents struggle to find the right match and expertise.

# 7

# REVISION STRATEGIES AND EXAM PREPARATION

We all have a preference for how we memorise facts and skills, and the best strategies for the individual take some exploring through practising. Students often don't know how to revise, either because they have been presented with a strategy that simply doesn't work for them, or they haven't been presented with any strategies at all. Students are often overwhelmed by the amount of information and topics they must learn and remember.

Make sure you plan a revision timetable with your student, or enhance the timetable given by the school. By creating a practical, working timetable you can alleviate the student's stress and give them back control of their learning. This is particularly important for students you know who have organisational difficulties. They typically demonstrate they need a timetable by having not completed work you have set for them in a timely or satisfactory way.

**Here are some techniques you can apply with your student:**

## Recount

Rather than just rewriting and paraphrasing facts into notes, prompt your student to verbally recount their knowledge. Teach your student to skim read their notes to see if they have forgotten any details of importance. You can see the gaps in their knowledge by the detail they miss. Using keywords and phrases can be a good way to memorise difficult information, as can creating acronyms. So, a classic example of memorising how to structure a persuasive piece of writing is the:

P.E.E. METHOD:

**Point, Explanation, and Evidence.**

You can take it one step further by using the acronym

**PEEL:**

**Point, Explanation, Evidence and Link** (reiterating your point by linking to the previous paragraph or statement).

Here is a very brief illustration of this strategy in action within a body paragraph of an essay:

**POINT** - Lady Macbeth is a powerful woman. **LINK** - In my previous paragraph we witnessed the build-up of Lady Macbeth's sway over her husband's thoughts and actions. **EXPLANATION** - She can suppress any feelings of guilt and empathy to convince her husband to commit murder in order to gain power. **EVIDENCE** - In her impassioned speech to Macbeth (Act 1, Scene 5), she motivates him to commit his first act of murder, "He that's coming must be provided for, and you shall put this night's great business into my dispatch, which shall to all our nights and days to come give solely sovereign sway and masterdom." **POINT** – Her ability to convince her husband to see murder as a step towards becoming King, proves her power. **LINK** - In the next paragraph we will explore her strength of conviction further through the specific words she chooses in her dialogue with Macbeth.

## Visual Techniques

Having visual representations of coursework can also aid in memorising important areas. Many students find that the process of creating mind maps can act as a reminder of coursework and provide a visually stimulating final product with all relevant information in the one place. Similarly, creating revision posters can act in the same way, as can placing post-it notes with essential keywords around a study area.

For other students, mindmaps simply do not work as their preference for organisation requires a linear list of points to remember and recall information. In history, timelines can be extremely effective to put events into context; however, one person may organise their timeline left to right, and others right to left, or up and down, or down and up. Some may even organise timelines diagonally. Once again, this comes down to preference, and you need to work out how your student naturally prefers to organise their information.

## Revising in Groups

For students who find it difficult to organise their revision time, organising a study group with friends can be beneficial. This may become an adjunct to your business. Meeting in a public place, such as a library, rather than your student's home may lessen distraction. Study groups make a student feel that they're not alone in their learning and peers can quickly learn collaboratively.

## Verbal techniques

Have your student prepare a presentation for you and teach it. When we teach, we learn to organise and think deeply about what we are learning, and the key points behind our learning. A student teaching to you, can help take the words and knowledge off the page so that they understand and articulate the concept in their own words. Ensure them that you are there to assist them through any sticking points. By verbalising, we use our own voice, and our brain works overtime to express the images in our mind.

## Active techniques

Express the concept by moving your body. There is no harm in a bit of acting to express a concept. Many of us learn a sequence of sports and dance movements best by moving until it becomes second nature, unlike others who can simply see a movement and replicate it. Kinaesthetic learning is more common than we realise, but many still do not teach by having their students express themselves through body movement. Think about how you could teach the order of a practical chemistry lesson by rehearsing the measurements and mixes of a formula. Movement is often the quickest way to teach socially awkward teens strategies to improve their social skills, by practising specific open body language.

Having worked in Private schools, I have seen students "spoon-fed" skills such as how to write a 5-paragraph essay. There is no harm in this method as we should all be taught skills, rather than being left to flounder about making errors and losing heart in our ability. Skills are skills and understanding concepts is the true knowledge we are aiming to teach. Mistakes can teach us lessons too, but not when the knowledge is beyond your understanding, and you are continually failing without support.

Here is an example where I illustrate a 5-paragraph essay as a worthy skill which you can teach quickly and effectively, down to the very number of sentences. Constraints are a good start to help your student rapidly progress in their skills. Further essay writing skills such as the use of definition, description, narrative, argument and persuasion, comparison and contrast, cause and effect, and the techniques of literary analysis can be taught as effective devices within this structure.

When writing a 5-paragraph essay, there are distinct elements to know and use:

· · ·

THE INTRODUCTION CONSISTS of around three to five sentences and typically requires an attention-grabbing hook of one to two sentences to capture the reader's attention and keep them reading. Hooks are often a rhetorical question, a quote from the text in study, a relevant fact, or statistic. You then follow-up with two or three sentences briefly outlining your supporting arguments without devolving too much information. You don't want to give away the complete argument. You finally finish your introduction with a thesis statement clearly identifying the topic discussed, and a direct response to the question asked.

THE THESIS STATEMENT is an essential part of your entire essay: this is your argument. This statement will be the basis for the rest of your essay.

IT IS OFTEN BETTER to write the body of your essay first, then follow-up with your conclusion and finally write your introduction. When you barrel into an introduction, sometimes your opinion changes as your write the body and you end up with an incongruent argument.

EACH BODY PARAGRAPH should be five to seven sentences.

Your opening paragraph should contain your strongest argument. "Save your best 'til first," is a twist on the old saying, "Save your best 'til last." You must keep your reader engaged.

Each body introduction should be one sentence where you briefly state your argument, without revealing too much. You follow up with evidence and an explanation contained within three to five sentences that fully support your argument.

The Concluding Sentence should be the opposite of the introduction. You are briefly concluding your argument and incorporating your main thesis, then linking into your next paragraph.

· · ·

ARGUE your paragraph body points in this order:

- First body paragraph: contains your strongest argument.
- Second body paragraph: contains your weakest argument.
- Third body paragraph: contains your most persuasive argument.

YOU CONCLUSION CONTAINS three to five sentences.

Restate your thesis conclusively within your first sentence.

Paraphrase your supporting arguments from your three body paragraphs combined within two or three sentences. Conclude with a hook sentence that may surprise the reader and sums things up in a few words, such as a rhetorical question.

**Exam Advice for Prepping your students:**

**Pre-preparation**

- Make sure you have practised past papers on the same subject and from the right examination board with your student. This will familiarise you with the format and desensitise your student's nervousness around the style of questions they will likely be asked.
- The more they practise similar questions, the better their answers will be, as long as you guide them to improve their answers.
- Inform both the student and their parents of the following:
- They need a good night's sleep. They should go to bed at the same time as usual, in the same routines. Set an alarm clock the night before.
- They should have a good breakfast in the morning. They

need to be hydrated and have been been to the toilet before the exam.

- Get to the exam early, rather than in a last-minute panic. Transport to the exam should be planned.
- They should read and rehearse their study notes before entering the exam hall to focus their minds on the subject and promote a confident mindset.
- Teach them how to take some deep breaths. It can help focus their attention.
- Prepare them to go in knowing that they can only do their best, and they must go out of their way to do their best.

**In the Exam**

- They must listen to and read the instructions.
- They should have all their pens, pencils, and ruler, ready and organised.
- They complete the cover sheet with their name and student information.
- They should focus on the page before them and practise blocking out all distractions. Use a spare piece of paper to cover everything on the exam except for the question they are answering.
- Look at the question. How many parts are there? The number of sentences or number of items in a list reflects how many areas need to be answered. If there is an indicator of the marks to the side of the question, look at them to decide the length and importance of the answer. A mark of 3 signifies there are 3 things needed in their answer. It may be a mix of facts, evidence such as quotes, 3 stages in working out a sum, or a language technique.
- They can use the spaces and working out areas to jot down ideas or methods to help answer the question. The answers to questions often occur in boxes that contain the

answer. Unless instructed otherwise, they can use the other spaces for formulating their response.

- Enhance their answers. Look for ways, such as quotes or related knowledge to answer their questions.
- If they have time at the end of the exam, make sure they look back to answer any questions they have missed, or any questions that deserve a better or more thorough answer. They might just pick up an extra point or two.

**After the exam**

They should relax for a while. Even if they have another exam coming up shortly, they should take a moment and congratulate themselves for doing their best.

If it is a mid-term paper, and they receive it back, ensure they go over it with you and revise any corrections. This will help them close gaps and improve their performance in their final assessments.

# 8

# UK 11+ 13+ INDEPENDENT SCHOOLS EXAMINATION BOARD PRE-TESTS

Schools that prepare students for examination boards are known as Preparatory schools or "prep" schools, preparing students to sit Common Entrance or Scholarship examinations in order to win a place in a selective independent school.

Pre-tests have recently increased as the demand and competition for places in top private schools has grown. More and more applications for independent schools are occurring across the UK, and pre-tests are used at ages 10 to 11 (Year 6 and 7), rather than at age 12 to 13 to assess whether a child matches the teaching style and culture of a particular school.

Children who are assessed as achieving a higher level are offered a place on condition of them passing the Common Entrance Examination sat in Year 8. Pretesting is and indicator and of academic achievement and does not replace Common Entrance, nor Scholarship exams, which must be sat.

Pretesting includes academic performance in maths, English and verbal and non-verbal reasoning. It is often inclusive of a mix of online and written testing, plus an individual or group interview. A child's personality is just as important as the academic assessment itself.

Some students who don't pass the pre-test but interview well are put on a reserve waiting list to replace those who do not accept a position at the school when offers are finally made.

For parents disappointed in this early testing approach, it's important for them to realise that it's better that their child fits in with their school rather than being at odds with its approaches and philosophies. There are plenty of great schools out there not reliant on such stringent testing. There is nothing worse for a child than having to see their performance fall behind their peers due to their parents' ambitions for them. An academic programme that is too challenging is not good for a child's self-esteem and confidence in their abilities.

## Components of pre-testing

The ISEB Common Pre-test is the most used and presents as an online, multiple-choice test in maths, English, Verbal and Non-Verbal Reasoning. There are four sections that last for a total of two and a half hours. This test typically occurs in the student's current school and the sections can be taken separately or as one long test. This is decided by the prep school running the test.

The ISEB Common Pre-test results are shared with all of the independent schools applied for by the parents or school and considers how young the applicant is and how early the test is taken.

Some schools create their own tests as a pre-test which are mostly printed papers rather than online. Other schools will also use a known assessment provider like Cambridge CEM Assessment or GL CAT4 cognitive assessments.

Online ISEB assessments are adaptive in the questions they present. Each new question presented is adapted to the student's response to the question they have just answered.

## Prepping a student

As a tutor, it is important to develop the following areas when preparing children for pre-tests and common entrance:

1. **Speed:** To complete the test within the required timeframes
2. **Concentration and Stamina:** To improve the student's ability to sit through long examination
3. **Familiarity and Resilience:** Exposure to the content and style of tests will improve your student's chances of success in a competitive examination. As dull as it may seem, it is the only way to prepare the student as a successful candidate. They are being prepared for a competition to win a place against dozens of others.
4. **Interview:** The results from the ISEB pre-test decide who is called back for interview.

Each school varies in approach, but all are geared to identify the right students for their school. It's absolutely essential to check each school's approach so your student is prepared properly for that school's approach. If you can't find the information on the website, call up admissions and ask. They may well be able to email or post you their dates and how they conduct their examination.

Maths and English questions often reflect the UK Key Stage 2 National Curriculum and will test skills and knowledge for this age group at a Level 4 or 5. Academic schools will expect a higher performance. Typically, a Year 6 child will be expected to work at a Level 6 which is expected in Year 7 and even 8. Students will typically read at an age and use vocabulary eighteen months to two years above their current age.

As verbal and non-verbal reasoning is not often taught in schools, you as a tutor will need to provide this practice.

You can find many resources in the form of past 11+ papers online for free.

Your student must get used to timed practice.

## The interview

A high score needs to be achieved in the tests to ensure a call back for interview. If the student is lucky enough to be called back for interview, this is the point when they need to shine and stand out from the others. The right attitude to education and life, the desire to learn and the student's personality needs to fit the school and the peers who attend.

The school will ask the potential student to meet a senior member of staff.

Interviews typically focus on a student's interests and the extra-curricular activities and hobbies they participate in. Asking about life experiences may also be brought up in interview. Other interviews might be focused on academic pursuits. Typically, all areas of the student's life are asked about to see how fluently they converse, how they solve problems and the vocabulary they use to express their thoughts. Thoughtfulness is typically the strongest trait as it reflects deeper thinking.

Interviews can be with the student only or the student may participate as part of a group. How the student performs and conducts themselves as part of a group is what the interviewer is observing.

Typically, questions will be asked that provoke a student response. A student must be able to back up their thoughts with a logical argument. There is no right or wrong, unless the mistake glaringly reflects a fault in the students thinking or understanding. To prepare for such an interview, the tutor and parents can help by entering open discussions to help build the student confidence and encourage the skills you find in a logical debate:

- Demonstrating knowledge on a topic
- Staying on topic
- Speaking clearly, and charismatically

- Being confident in their opinion
- Making a point and backing it up with evidence
- Using confident and positive body language
- Using a true story to make a point
- Asking for clarification. Never lying when they don't know

Students are often asked about what they're reading, and the student should be able to freely describe and discuss a book, its character, it's theme, setting and language techniques used.

## Reports and References

The headteacher of the student's school is often required for a reference from the independent school that the student is applying for. It is confidential and you as a tutor, and the parent will not be able to view it.

Headteacher at preparatory school will work hard to produce a quality reference and compose it to suit the school that the student is applying for. They will highlight the student's strengths and honestly report any academic and other achievements, plus any welfare concerns. A headteacher will quickly gain a poor reputation with selective schools if their references do not accurately match the students they are referring.

As the student's tutor you must encourage their confidence in their abilities. This means ensuring they understand mathematical concepts, grammar, spelling and punctuation. They must have practised all types of questions that could come up and know how to identify and answer these questions. They must be given experience with both the online and offline tests.

It is important that your students begin this preparation eighteen months to a year before sitting their exam.

Encourage them to read a number of age-appropriate books, teach them how to express their own opinion on topics and have a knowledge of current news. Teach them to present themselves confidently.

. . .

FOLLOW this link for resources for testing:
    https://piacademy.co.uk


**BELOW IS a list of a number of ISEB pretest UK schools:**
Bedford School, Charterhouse, Easton Square Upper School, Hurstpierpoint College, Northfields Int. High School, St Paul's School, Wellington College, Bradfield College, Cheltenham College, Eton College, Marlborough College, Palmers Green High School, St Swithun's School, Westminster School, Brighton College, City of London School, Harrow School, Monkton Combe School, Radley College, Stowe School, Wetherby Senior School, Caterham School, Dauntsey's School, Headington School, Mount Kelly College, Reddam House School, University College School, Worth School


**A GROUP of London schools use the 11+ London Consortium test, which is a test taken that feeds into all of the following schools:**
Channing School, Francis Holland School, Regent's Park, Francis Holland School Sloane Square, Godolphin and Latymer, More House School, Northwood College for Girls, Notting Hill and Ealing High School, Queen's College London, South Hampstead High School, St Helen's School London, St James Senior Girls' School


**OTHER SCHOOLS USE their own specific pretests:**
Alleyn's School, Ampleforth College, Charterhouse, City of London School for Boys, Downside School, Dulwich College, Emanuel School, Eton, Hampton, Harrodian, Harrow, King's College School, Wimbledon, Marlborough, Merchant Taylor's School, Radley College, Sevenoaks School, St Paul's, Stowe, The King's School, Canterbury, Tonbridge School, UCS Hampstead, Wellington, Westminster, Wetherby Senior School, Winchester College

Unfortunately, you cannot access any online ISEB common entrance past papers; the closest you will get to this is the ISEB familiarisation test,

HTTPS://TESTWISE.TESTINGFORSCHOOLS.COM/TESTS/PLAYER-DEMO-ISEB/#/

Further information on the ISEB can be found on their site:

https://www.iseb.co.uk/Schools/General-information/Common-Pre-Tests

# 9

# COMMUNICATING WITH PARENTS

When speaking with the student's parents/guardians, be honest but encouraging by offering solutions to improve their child's learning.

Parents are keen to know how your session with their child went. It's vital to keep parents, and the school when required, up to date with their progress and is part of a holistic approach to teaching.

Always catch the parents after lessons and let them know what the lesson's focus was. If you must leave in a hurry, promise them you will email them feedback on the session. Highlight all the positives of the session and let them know the areas you intend focusing on next time.

Create a progress report to show parents. It will help the parents be involved in revising the material you've covered through your lessons so far. Give them a sense of where your student is positioned in their age group. Are they working towards their peers age-group? Working at the level of their peers? Or working above their peers?

Be honest with parents when discussing a student's progress. Praise and give constructive criticism on how their child can improve their knowledge or performance. You don't want to disappoint anyone by over-promising or over-estimating their child's ability or giving any information that is simply not accurate. You can always say to a parent you need time to formulate a proper report of how their child is doing, if they are putting pressure on you for a response.

Being overly critical of a student's work will only bring negative responses. Always reframe criticism in a positive light with a solution-focused response of suggested learning or activities. Be specific about exactly where their performance is lacking and what can be done about it.

Parents must not pin all their hopes on you as a tutor because you have over-promised your impact or results you can achieve. The student must also be trying, and the parents must be supporting them.

You are considered the expert in your subject, and you need to feedback as an expert. Avoid predicting a student's possible performance in school or an exam until you know the student well enough. At some point you'll know more when you test them with material similar to the school they attend or wish to attend.

Sometimes parents will say that their child needs a particular result from your tutoring to pursue future schooling or a career. Be honest, and feedback only what you have observed and the commitment and knowledge that is required by their child to meet the results needed for that school or career.

## Have clear Terms and Conditions

Have a clear Terms and Conditions document, stating that although you will give your full efforts, you cannot guarantee that students will attain their desired grades. This isn't a reflection of your tutoring ability but a number of circumstances that may be beyond your control; including: the parent and child's commitment, ability, amount of tutoring, and enough time allowed for preparation.

You want to have a friendly but professional relationship with your client, built on trust and honesty. They are your employer.

**Safety Advice when tutoring**

Always let someone know where you are going when you are out and about tutoring. As a solo tutor, you don't have the backup of your workplace tracking where you are at all times. Have a timetable accessible to a family member with all the addresses of where you are tutoring for each timed slot.

If you have any concerns about a tutoring placement, let someone know when you've arrived at your destination and how long you intend on being in the property. Likewise, let someone know when you have left your destination.

If you are concerned about a student or parent or concerned about the area where you will be tutoring, don't go. You will have a sense if things just don't add up or seem right. If possible, have someone close drop you off and wait for you to finish.

Carry a mobile phone with you but do not bring it out while you're tutoring. Never take photographs of children or details of children, such as their name, address, or any other contact information such as email addresses. You can take photographs of your student's work if the parent or guardian gives you permission.

Look into lone worker safety. Visit the Suzy Lamplugh Trust website or follow this link to the UK Government Guidelines for Lone Workers: https://www.hse.gov.uk/lone-working/worker/index.htm

For the USA, visit this site for further information, but take note that Lone worker policy varies from state to state, and most information comes from Private Companies selling GPS logging and emergency Apps: https://www.totalsafety.com/lone-worker-protection/

PART II

# BE OUTSTANDING IN ONLINE TUTORING AND ZOOM

10

---

# USING ZOOM TO MAXIMISE YOUR ONLINE TUTORING

Zoom features can help you to direct various kinds of interactive tasks for one student or many more. Presenting a variety of tasks through different Zoom features gives you the ability to break up a long session and present content in a multitude of different and engaging ways.

## A quick Zoom overview

Zoom is a web-based video conferencing tool with a local, desktop client and a mobile app that allowing users to meet online. Basic Zoom accounts are free and sync up with Google. It takes less than a few minutes to sign-up.

The host always controls the meeting, which is to your complete advantage as a tutor. Even if you grant students the ability to share, you can quickly halt that ability if they don't abide by what is commonly known as 'Zoom etiquette.' A student is an invitee in a meeting that you have scheduled. A student doesn't require a Zoom account to join a meeting, and the free plan allows up to 100 students, for up to 40 minutes. Tutoring one student is free for an unlimited amount of time, with all the features you require to teach effectively.

## Tips for your technology when using any online video conferencing platform

You may not wish to outlay any money until you have started to bring in an income. The following tips will improve your tutoring experience for your student ten-fold. They will however only enhance good teaching, not cover up poor teaching.

1. The most important aspect of teaching online is having a stable and reliable Internet connection. No internet, no lesson! You can link your device to your phone data allowance and use that in a pinch. Depending on your phone provider plan, this could prove to be extremely costly.
2. Ensure your web camera is at eye level. If it's slightly above, you will look submissive. If it's slightly below, you will look authoritarian and threatening. Eye level creates an equal connection. If you are using a laptop camera, raise your laptop camera to eye level and use a separate Bluetooth keyboard and mouse to input.
3. Light yourself from the front, or use natural lighting, such as a window. An adjustable cool to warm LED ring light, will even your face and reduce shadows, giving you a softer, non-threatening appearance.
4. You can also use white sheets of paper to reflect natural or artificial light evenly on both sides of your face. A white or off-white Chinese paper lantern hung in front of you also gives off a perfect soft, even light.
5. Light the wall behind you with any lamp pointed at it to separate you from your background. It will give a 3-Dimensional effect to your online session, rather than making you appear as flat as a pancake.
6. Ensure your microphone enhances your voice. A tinny sounding microphone distances you from your student

and is often what you have in a laptop or desktop setup. Ensure your microphone is of decent quality to reproduce your voice. You may have great lighting and you might appear perfect on the camera; however, sound is often more important than video when teaching. A USB microphone will plug straight into your device, and I suggest an easy-to-use microphone, such as a Blue Yeti Professional. Your other options are to choose a headphone and microphone all-in-one set, lapel microphone or decent pair of earbuds with a good microphone. The only way to test the equipment you already possess is to Zoom call a friend or family member and ask for feedback as you speak to them.

7. It is quite difficult to draw and write with a mouse unless you are well practised. Use a drawing tablet and pen that plugs into your device, so that you can write and draw on the Zoom whiteboard. Wacom produce a decent base-level drawing tablet which is easy to carry about and set up. You can also use an interactive screen tablet, such as android, Microsoft or Apple, with the Zoom app loaded on it for direct writing and drawing, but it will take a little research for you to set up. Alternatively, you can connect your apple iPad to your laptop as a drawing/writing tablet, wired or wireless, using "Sidecar" display.

8. If your built-in webcam is of poor quality, invest in a decent brand of webcam, such as Logitech, or an equivalent that produces the minimum of HD (High Definition) image to 4K or more. Check reviews for the quality of the image, and if it includes a built-in microphone, the quality of sound.

## Zoom classroom management

As an online tutor you must be able to manage your virtual class. There are moments when online tutoring is not that dissimilar to turning your back on your class in a physical classroom setting. When you have more than one student, you need to keep your eyes open.

**Some areas that you need to monitor are:**

Ensuring you enable "Waiting room" so that you only allow student entry and not the entry of anyone outside of your invitation. Never publicly display a Zoom invitation unless you intend to and are presenting to a group over the age of 18.

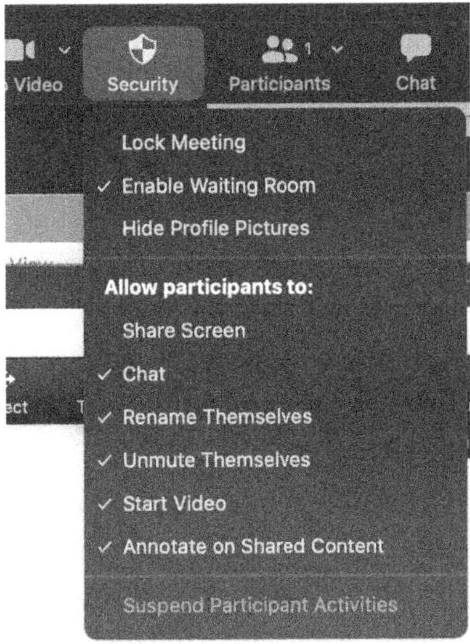


*Waiting Room*

ENSURING you can always see your students. This means that they must have their video on, so you can monitor they are behaving appropriately. If there are multiple attendees, some may be hidden on the next page of video images.

Ensuring you can always see Zoom chat and enable or disable it if chat becomes inappropriate.

Ensuring that you know how to terminate a participant if their behaviour is inappropriate.

Ensuring that you know if you see or hear any illegal activity, you **must** report it to the appropriate authorities in your city, town, or country.

HERE I OUTLINE a variety of recommendations for beginning each online class. This guideline will help you prevent possible safeguarding issues or inappropriate behaviours.

ASK participants to rename themselves appropriately, first name only. If they don't know how, you can go into the "Security" setting and do it for them. Don't allow them to later rename themselves within the session. In the "Security" setting make sure that under "Allow participants to:" you untick "Rename Themselves." Only their first names and no attention seeking, or inappropriate names should be displayed by the student.

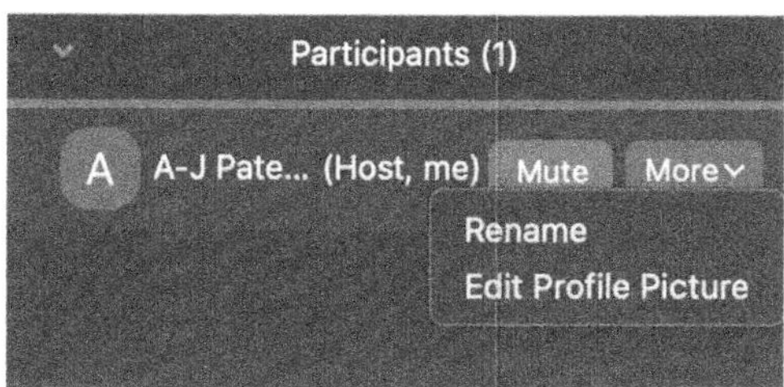


*Rename*

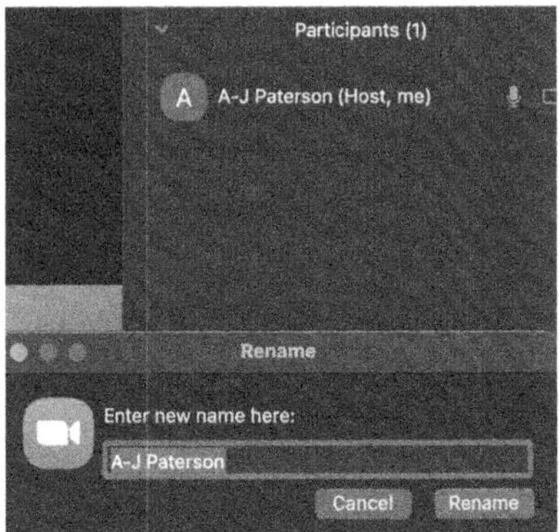

*Just type in the student's first name only*

LOCK the meeting

Immediately lock your meeting as soon as your student has joined or have a 5-to-10-minute deadline before locking a multiple-participant session, to prevent outsider intrusion. In the "Security" setting make sure you click "Lock Meeting" at the top of the choices.

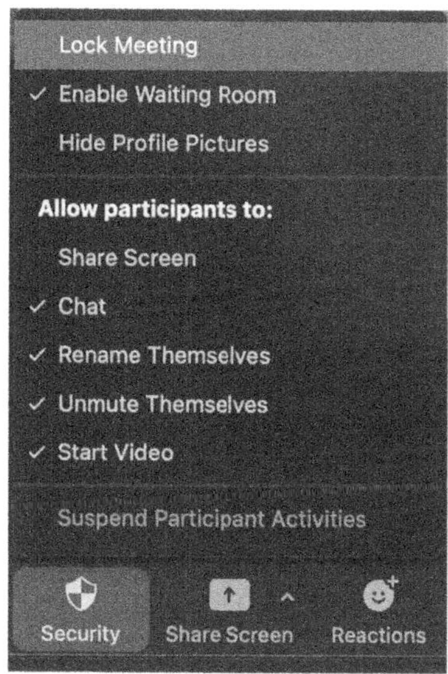

*Lock Meeting*

Don't allow the participants to screen share.

In the "Security" setting under "Allow participants to:" untick "Share screen." You can allow "Share screen" when you know and trust your student, and they have something important to share.

End the meeting for students/parents who don't follow the rules

If needed, remove people from the room. On the Participants menu, you can mouse over a participant's name and several options will appear, including "Remove." Click to remove someone from the meeting. Follow-up with a phone call or email to explain their breach of "etiquette."

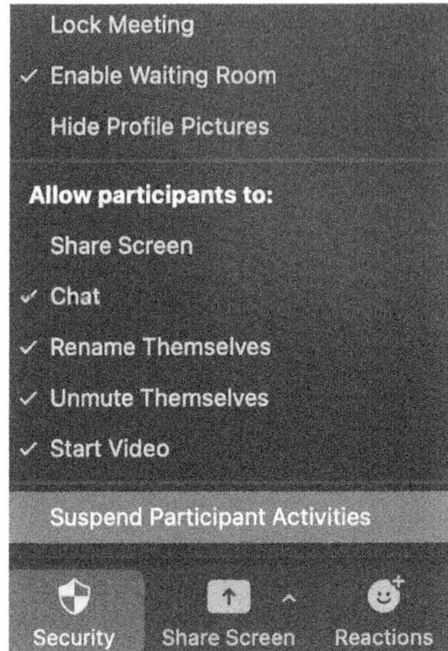

*Suspend Participant*

END the meeting properly by "End Meeting for All," not by clicking "Leave Meeting." If you just leave the meeting, all the other attendees will still be present, without your supervision. You want to ensure that students are not still connected with one another under your meeting where there could be the opportunity for inappropriate behaviour.

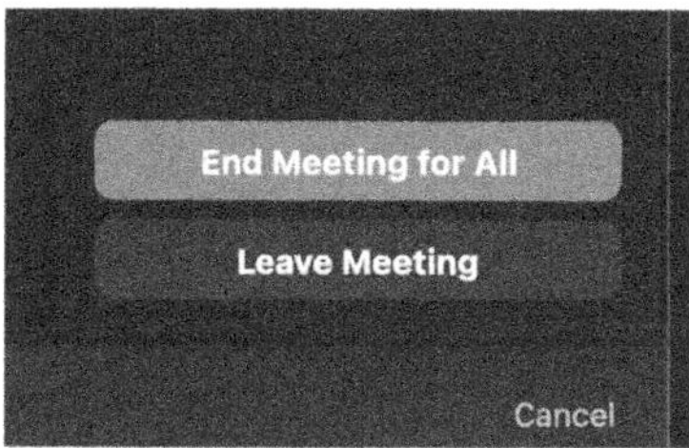

*Correctly end the meeting*

WHEN USING CHAT, at the bottom of the chat window, click the 3 dots and then click who you want your student to interact with, typically "Everyone." You can always click "No one" if their chat behaviour is inappropriate.

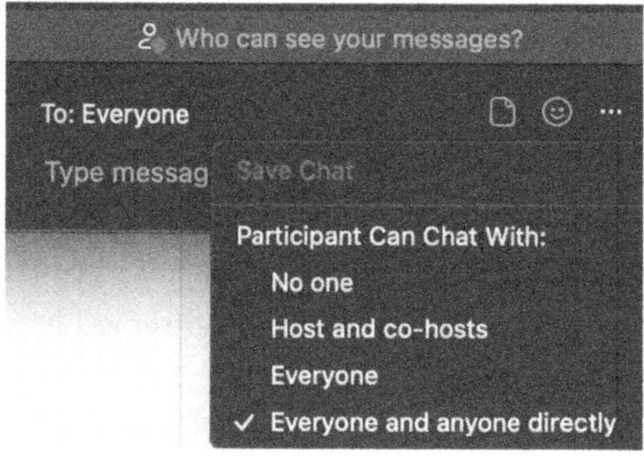

*Chat options*

FINALLY, here are a couple of things for you to carry out before a session.

- Test your session video and sound in a solo meeting prior to going live. A test meeting is started, simply by going to

the opening screen and choosing 'New Meeting' and not inviting anyone to join.
- Turn off chat, participants' screen share, annotation, etc. in your Zoom settings, until you know your student/s understand your rules for chat, sharing and annotation.

## Zoom participant etiquette

The following participant expectations should be the norm. Students and parents who don't follow these guidelines can be removed from the Zoom meeting under your established rules.

- Mute your microphone if you aren't talking.
- No virtual backgrounds are allowed.
- Ensure your natural background has no personal items, inappropriate items or features that identify your location or personal identification.
- Use your real name and ensure it is your first name only.
- Be on time.
- Only post chat messages relevant to the lessons.
- Only share materials that the tutor has approved.
- Do not turn your Video off unless directed by your tutor.

These expectations are very similar to what you would expect in the classroom. Be on time for class, wait your turn to talk, and keep your discussion on topic, without distracting others.

## Professional development

There are courses and advisors who can help you to learn effective online tutoring, including the advising services on offer at miniteaching.com

You can practise with friends and family, simply by inviting them to Zoom sessions and exploring the features. These features will be explained further in the next chapter.

In Conclusion, always remember that you as the host have full control over everything on Zoom, and this puts you in a safe position.

# 11

# ZOOM FEATURES TO ENHANCE LEARNING

## CHAT

Using chat encourages interaction and discussion as students can connect with their ideas and suggestions without disrupting the main class. In chat, students can individually ask questions and even share content and send responses. You too can send PDF's and documents of work and tasks, separate to your main teaching on camera. It's like handing out a worksheet, explanation, or other text in a physical classroom.

Chat enables posts to be delivered to the whole class or directly to a particular user. Ensure that if chat is enabled for your students, that you set it so that they can only chat in the main chat window and no personal chats can occur. If you want to keep a record of chats, particularly if inappropriate student chat has occurred, you can access the complete chat history of the lesson.

You can also use chat for group-thinking and brainstorming sessions. One technique is to group students in small groups in break-out rooms. Invite one student to be "chair" and collate a summary of their group's contributions. However, you won't be able to monitor what occurs in a break-out room unless you assign a responsible adult to be part of the group. You can enter the breakout group whenever you like and disband the group to bring them back into the main presentation again.

## SCREEN SHARING AND ANNOTATION

Zoom has annotation capability to write down or illustrate an idea for your student/s. When using a shared screen or the shared whiteboard, use the drawing toolbar to 'Annotate' while viewing the display. Access to this tool is under the control of the host, so participants are treated as screen readers unless given permission to use annotation tools. You can allow this ability for a participant by opening the security settings and ticking 'Annotate on Shared Content.' This is when having a drawing tablet comes in extra handy. You can write with more accuracy compared with just using your mouse. A USB plug-in drawing tablet and pen takes a little practise but can quickly be mastered. This is when you should practise drawing on the Zoom whiteboard by setting up a "fake" meeting, i.e., starting a new meeting with no participants and clicking share to access the whiteboard.

Sharing screens is very important for enhancing your teaching skills and engaging multisensory learning. Sharing a screen with Zoom is simple; all you do is press on the "Share Screen" link at the bottom of your conference. You will then press on the device you would like to display. The share capability, and what you convey on the whiteboard, makes Zoom an exceptional tool for teaching and illustrating your concepts quickly and efficiently.

Share documents, and live footage from your side of the camera. You can use the camera on your smart phone as a visualiser to show real text from a book, and even use the magnifying glass on your smart phone to zoom in on an experiment you may have set up for science. When you share your screen as a visualiser, choose your phone cable-connected to your desktop or laptop and turn your camera on, hovering over the text to display it live to your student/s.

## Responsibility and Duty of Care Online

Fostering engagement with your students is critical to success in distance learning, it's not difficult for your student to be watching a video or engaging in social media on their phone or screen alongside your lesson.

It's nearly impossible to instil classroom discipline to the same degree in an online setting as a physical classroom. What's to stop an unmotivated student from logging into your session but passively ignoring you if they aren't concerned about consequences.

Parental responsibility is to be encouraged so their child is held accountable for accessing the lesson and participating. An unsupportive parent may require you to assert your right as a professional to withdraw your services if no headway is gained in student participation or commitment to learning. Sending a set of guidelines or expectations for distance learning, is required for your sanity.

Sooner or later, you will encounter a non-participative or difficult student. However, also expect a wide range of commitment levels from parents. In the end, there's little that can be done beyond a parent-tutor call to address the fact that they are paying money for little educational reward. You can hold the student and parent to account to the guidelines you send home or use them to warn them of the commitment required to succeed.

Ultimately, you must win your student's attention by inspiring them and engaging their curiosity. However, you also need to know when the student is just not ready for tutoring despite your efforts.

Always involve the parents, even more than you would ordinarily, particularly with younger students. Let them know exactly the content of the lesson and walk them quickly through a concept you taught in the session. Inform them of their child's commitment and concentration, and especially highlight their achievements.

Beyond parental information, the student's latest school report reflects their performance, effort, and behaviour, and should become your primary source for closing gaps in their learning or providing the challenges needed for the student to progress. Performance in the classroom, homework and test/exam scores are the most common components of a grade or level, alongside their personal and social capabilities. It's important to have access to this information wherever possible.

Never expect the same commitment in a virtual classroom as in a physical classroom, without building up some expectations first, and establishing the student's comfort with your delivery and their trust in you. Remember the 3 T's – Things Take Time. Even adults struggle to adapt to working virtually from home. If teaching the student seems difficult, communicate to the parent why and what may help them to engage. You may have the parent sitting next to them to get them started.

Be aware that there are adults who will put their children's comments and complaints above any advice you might offer them. Some parents will even offer up excuses for their child. These can be the parents who first and foremost wish to please their children, rather than challenge them or teach them responsibility or resilience, because it is easier. They interfere with your student's progress, despite your advice, and will continue to jump in whenever their child even feels slightly uncomfortable. Parents like this are very difficult to work for, and luckily are rare.

## LIVE STREAMS

Though I don't recommend this approach for students under the age of 18, if you are confident about your teaching, live streaming is available. Live streaming is a feature that lets you Zoom broadcast in real-time to other media platforms, such as YouTube, Facebook, and more. Live streams can be enabled for both regular meetings and webinars but require an account of Pro or higher. To enable live-streaming, as an admin you can log onto Zoom's website and go to Account Management > Account Settings > In Meeting (Advanced) > "Allow live-streaming the meetings."

You then check the streaming services you wish to be able to use. For webinars, this can be done via the Account Management >

Webinar Settings > Edit. To use a custom streaming service, check that option, then provide a Stream URL, a Page URL, and a Stream Key where you're prompted for instructions, so hosts will be able to use that custom option should they wish.

This approach is difficult to monitor and to prevent outsiders entering the session. It may however prove of benefit for those presenting their services to prospective parents through social media.

## How to Set Up a Zoom Meeting/Session

Here's a step-by-step guide to set up a Zoom meeting easily:

**For Desktop**

To start a zoom meeting, log in to your zoom account, select the 'Host a meeting' tab, the following options will surface: "With Video on," "With Video off," and "Screen share only." Choose the appropriate option.

You will be redirected to the zoom app where the meeting can start. Here you can take note of the invitation URL that attendees will need to gain access to the meeting.

To invite your participants, select the "Invite" button in the new meeting screen. You get the option of inviting your participants using a URL or Invitation, this can be sent via an instant message, email, or text.

An email containing the meeting details can be sent to the participants via your chosen email client.

**For Mobile Devices**

Log into your zoom app, click the 'New meeting' icon, edit the meeting settings in line with the options that suit you. After that, click on the 'Start a Meeting' button. To add participants, tap the 'Participants' icon once the meeting starts, once the participant menu opens, select the "Invite tab." Then, you can share the meeting details through email, text, and instant messages.

## HOW TO JOIN A ZOOM MEETING

To join using a meeting link, click on the link or if using a web browser, copy and paste

To join Using a Meeting ID, log into your zoom app, select the "Join" button, input the meeting ID and your display name for the meeting, tap the "Join" button.

You can now start your meeting with your partners.

## HOW TO SCHEDULE MEETINGS

Important meetings can be forgotten when you have a tight schedule.

With Zoom, however, you can schedule meetings beforehand to avoid this. This can be done by setting the meeting date and time, providing a meeting ID, ascertaining whether it needs a password to join or not.

### For Desktop

Go to the zoom app and tap on the "Schedule button." Next, you input the meeting details in the "Schedule meeting" icon that appears. Its date and time, privacy, and access setting can be inputted.

When you're done adjusting, tap the "Schedule" button at the bottom right of the screen.

### For Mobile

Log into the Zoom app, go to the "Meet and Chat" page, and select "Schedule." Input the meeting name, time, and date, then tap done. You can save this to your calendar as a reminder.

## HOW TO RECORD ZOOM MEETINGS

This feature allows you to document meetings in virtual form and it's indispensable in groups who use Zoom as their major tool for communication.

These recordings can be saved to your device or Zoom cloud where every member of the team can access it

Here's how to record Zoom meetings:

**For Desktop**

Once the meeting starts, click on the "Record" icon, you'll have two options, to record on the computer or to record to the cloud, to stop the recording, simply click on Pause/stop recording. Alternatively, ending the meeting automatically stops the recording. After the meeting, the recording can be saved to your preferred storage and archived where it can be retrieved at any point in time.

**For Mobile**

On mobile devices, Zoom lets you save meeting recordings only to the Zoom Cloud. Here's how to record a Zoom meeting from your mobile. Here, you only have the option of saving recordings to Zoom cloud. Once the meeting starts, click on the 'More' option, select the 'Record to the cloud' to begin recording. You can pause or stop recording by tapping the 'More' button. After the meeting, the recording is saved to the folder 'My Recordings.

# PART III

# BE OUTSTANDING IN THE TUTORING BUSINESS

**12**

---

# TAX MATTERS UK

When you become self-employed, you must register with HMRC. Technically, as soon as you receive your first payment for your private tuition services, you must declare those earnings and all further earnings at the end of the Tax Year. Failing to register as self-employed will result in you being fined.

## How to Register as a Self-Employed Private Tutor

The easiest way to register as self-employed is to do so online. By completing a registration form, you are making HMRC aware that you are now working for yourself, and you then become responsible for keeping track of your income and your expenses.

Once you are registered as self-employed, you will be sent a Self-Assessment Tax Return every year after the 5th of April which will instruct you on how to declare your earnings for the previous year. You will also be informed of deadline dates for when you need to return the form. If you choose to complete the form online, you are normally given an extended deadline. Once your form is submitted, you will then be contacted by HMRC and told how much income tax you owe for the tax period in question.

## Paying National Insurance Contributions

Being self-employed means paying your own Class 2 National Insurance contributions (NICs) and if you earn over a certain threshold, you also need to pay Class 4 contributions. It is possible to defer your National Insurance payments, and depending on low earnings, you may be exempt from paying National Insurance. To find out if this applies to you, contact HMRC for further guidance and information.

## Paying Value Added Tax (VAT)

If you are earning over a certain amount, you may also be eligible for paying VAT on the services that you provide. You typically must be earning more than £70,000 per annum before registering to pay. It's possible to register for VAT voluntarily.

## Completing a Self-Assessment Tax Return

As a tutor, you must declare any earnings you make to HMRC as you would with any other employment, regardless of whether you work full-time or part-time.

Self-Assessment tax return forms are issued to those registered as self-employed, every April, covering the previous 12 months (i.e., the tax year to the 5th of April just passed).

To ensure the process is as stress-free as possible, keep and record all the information you require beforehand. Keep all paperwork up to date. Legally, everyone who is self-employed must keep records of their income.

Information that you may need before you begin completing your Self-Assessment form:

Records of your income and anything you can claim as expenditure or expenses

If you have PAYE employment as well as being self-employed, you will need details of any pay received from your employer

Information on 'other income' including investments, savings, pensions, and details of any capital gains

Your P60 which shows the tax you've paid having worked on the payroll of an employer, in the tax year (6 April to 5 April)

**Your bank statements or access to your online banking account**

Self-Employed in More Than One Job?

You'll need to fill in some additional pages on the tax return form. The supplementary pages - SA103S or SA103F, provide a space for you to declare any earnings you have gained from other jobs where you are self-employed.

The main form that you need to complete is called SA100. There are guidance notes to help you throughout the form and they tell you which parts you need to complete depending on your circumstances.

HMRC normally send you the forms you need and the guidance notes by post, however, you can also download the forms from the HMRC website.

Any tax that you owe must be paid by 31 January

Missing deadline dates can incur a £100 penalty, regardless of whether you have taxes to pay or not.

HMRC's Self-Assessment helpline is 0845 9000 444. You can also search online for "HMRC's Guide to Filling in Your Tax Return." https://www.gov.uk/self-assessment-forms-and-helpsheets

# TAX MATTERS USA

## Self-employment as a tutor in the USA

America's tax deadline is April 15.

Freelance tutors are part of the 10 percent of Americans who are self-employed.

If you're running your own tutoring business and not working for an agency or other employer, you're self-employed. Even if you tutor part-time and you have another full-time job.

Being self-employed classifies you as a 1099 independent contractor.

Form 1099 is different to the W-2 form employees receive from their place of work.

As an independent contractor no one is withholding taxes or making deductions on your behalf, so you must complete or hire a tax accountant to complete your tax form.

Because no one is taking money out of your earnings, set aside a portion of each paycheck. It is suggested that you save between 25 to 30 percent and set up a separate bank account for that cash reserve.

As a freelance tutor subject to the highs and lows of running your own business, savings come in handy if you encounter a dry spell or a financial emergency. This is known as an emergency fund, and I outline further information under the Budgeting chapter.

Independent contractors don't benefit from employer-sponsored health insurance. For freelance tutors with no full-time employer, explore the federal Marketplace (https://www.healthcare.gov/self-employed/coverage/) and set aside earnings to pay for it.

## Record your business expenses

Independent contractors can write off business expenses, so keep records and receipts for anything you spend toward your tutoring business. This includes resources, marketing costs, work-related phone and internet bills, and anything else you use in the daily running of your business.

## MISC

In some situations, independent contractors may need to collect and submit 1099-MISC (https://www.irs.gov/pub/irs-pdf/f1099msc.pdf) forms from a business entity you are tutoring for, such as an agency or school. If you've collected more than $600 from them in a calendar year, you'll need to keep the 1099-MISC.

But if your client is an individual student or parent who pays you directly, the 1099-MISC requirement is waived.

Discuss this with your clients before any tutoring as you need to collect completed 1099-MISC forms and submit them to the IRS by January 31.

## Quarterly Payments

Independent contractors who pay more than $1,000 in taxes in a calendar year must make estimated tax payments each quarter.

This means four payments, due on April 15, June 15, September 15, and January 15 (the following year). Paying on time is important, as missing a payment incurs penalty interest.

After a year of tutoring, look at your total taxes from the previous year to estimate how much you're likely going to owe this tax year. The IRS won't penalize you for using that number to estimate your quarterly payments.

If your total yearly earnings are less than $400, you won't need to make any quarterly payments, but you may still be required to file an income tax return. Check out page 7 of Form 1040 (https://www.irs.gov/pub/irs-pdf/i1040gi.pdf) to see if you meet any additional filing requirements.

## Deductions

As independent contractors, freelance tutors can claim several business-related deductions:

### 1. Your home office

If you conduct all or part of your tutoring business at home, you may be eligible for a home office deduction, regardless of whether you rent or own your home. Your home office must be the most used space for your tutoring business and used only for business.

You can still claim other business-related activities outside of the home, such as tutoring off-site, if your home office is used significantly.

The IRS offers a simplified option (https://www.irs.gov/businesses/small-businesses-self-employed/simplified-option-for-home-office-deduction ) for calculating your home office deductions.

If you're using a co-working space, you can deduct 100 percent of your co-working office rent off your taxes.

### 2. Transportation

If transportation was for business purposes (say for a meeting or client session at a library), you can claim it. You cannot however claim commuting to and from your place of work, such as your home office or co-working space.

For personal vehicle deduction check helpful guide to navigating your transportation deductions (https://www.irs.gov/publications/p463)

### 3. Business-related resources and courses

You can deduct any resources purchased and used directly for your tutoring business. If you use those resources in your personal life as well, you can only deduct the percentage of time that resource is used for your business.

RESOURCES INCLUDE:

- Stationary, such as books, pens, and pencils etc.
- Educational software
- Courses for you or your students
- Business software, such as accounting and tax
- Hardware such as computers and tablets
- Advertising, marketing, and promotional costs

### 4. Eating out and entertaining

You can deduct those meals and snacks directly related to your tutoring business, like a meeting at a cafe with a client to discuss your services.

### 5. Phone and Internet

You can deduct phone and internet costs that are directly related to your business. If you use your phone for personal calls and your internet for personal browsing, you can only claim a part of your business activities as a business-related percentage.

14

# RETIREMENT

This is a very short chapter as retirement plans should be discussed with expert financial advisors. The following are the two most obvious and common plans for both US and UK retirement.

## Independent retirement accounts

Freelance tutors without full-time employment won't have access to an employer-offered retirement account or pension (unless you had previous full-time employment). As independent contractors, freelance tutors can set up their own retirement accounts.

In the US you can set up an
independent 401(k) plan (https://www.irs.gov/retirement-plans/one-participant-401k-plans.)

Unlike traditional IRAs with a yearly maximum contribution of $5,500 ($6,500 for over 50), in your independent 401(k), you can defer the first $18,000 of your annual income ($24,000 for those over 50), plus an additional 25 percent of your annual salary up to a maximum of $53,000. You can even use some of your retirement savings for your business. There is a lot of paperwork that accompanies an independent 401(k) plan.

A POPULAR ALTERNATIVE is a SIMPLE IRA (https://www.irs.gov/retirement-plans/plan-sponsor/simple-ira-plan) with a maximum annual pre-tax contribution of $12,500 ($15,500 for over 50).

IN THE UK, you can invest in ISA's (https://www.gov.uk/individual-savings-accounts/how-isas-work)

or take out an independent pension plan. There are some suggestions here (https://www.thetimes.co.uk/money-mentor/article/best-ready-made-personal-pension/) for independent Pension plans.

ULTIMATELY, if you can afford the expense, investigate your retirement possibilities by speaking to a private Financial Advisor specialising in retirements and pensions. If tax is an issue for you, invest in a tax accountant and request that your appointment is in person. As you are paying for their time, you can ask all the questions you need and get a good education on what you must provide and what you can claim. As tax rules varies slightly from year to year, a tax accountant makes a very good investment.

15

# BUDGETING

Finances can seem daunting to most of us. In this chapter, I outline the basics of budgeting, covering the most important aspects that you should follow. Blindly guessing at what you are earning, and spending is a recipe for financial disaster. You need a plan and a way of tracking your earnings and expenditure, which you revisit frequently.

## A Small business budget

A small business budget is a financial plan providing your business with information considering capital, revenue, and expenditure.

Budgets convey an estimation of revenues and expenses over time, typically monthly or annually. They determine how and where to best spend your money.

BEGIN with knowing what your Startup Costs are, such as the following. This sheet includes both large and small business categories.

**Startup Costs**

Your company name

Date

| Item Cost | # of Months | Monthy Cost | Total Cost |
|---|---|---|---|
| **MONTHLY COSTS** | | | |
| Accounting Fees | | | |
| Employee Payroll Taxes and Benefits | | | £0.00 |
| Employee Salaries | | | £0.00 |
| Insurance | | | £0.00 |
| Interest | | | £0.00 |
| Legal Fees | | | £0.00 |
| Ongoing Advertising/Promotion | | | £0.00 |
| Rent/Lease Payments | | | £0.00 |
| Staff Salaries | | | £0.00 |
| Subcriptions | | | £0.00 |
| Supplies | | | £0.00 |
| Utilities | | | £0.00 |
| Miscellaneous | | | £0.00 |
| **TOTAL MONTHLY COSTS** | | | **£0.00** |
| **SINGLE COSTS** | | | |
| Advertising/Promotion | | | £0.00 |
| Business Licenses/Permits/Fees | | | £0.00 |
| Business Registration | | | £0.00 |
| Cash-On-Hand (Working Capital) | | | £0.00 |
| Consultant(s) | | | £0.00 |
| Furniture | | | £0.00 |
| Inventory | | | £0.00 |
| Machinery and Equipment | | | £0.00 |
| Software | | | £0.00 |
| Website Design & Development | | | £0.00 |
| Miscellaneous | | | £0.00 |
| **TOTAL ONE-TIME COSTS** | | | **£0.00** |
| **TOTAL STARTUP COSTS** | | | **£0.00** |

*Know all your startup costs*

## YOUR BUDGET SHOULD:

- Forecast your earnings through revenue, sales, and profit.
- Plan your business expenditure so you have a business-focused purpose behind everything you spend.
- Hold your spending accountable so you're actually meeting your desired goals and reaching forecasted milestones.

A SMALL BUSINESS budget must be re-evaluated frequently to ensure it aligns with your business needs and your continual goals.

Without an awareness of your projected cash flow, you can't plan the growth of your business.

## Creating a small business budget

Business budgets stop you from spending money in the wrong places and determine if your business costs are essential or optional. You might initially invest too heavily, getting into difficulties if you don't earn enough revenue to remain afloat. A budget provides a clear picture of your finances to spend at the right time, in the right way.

If you're hoping to get funding or raise capital through banks or investors, you will require a detailed business plan that includes a budget, so they have a clear picture of your forecasted spending. When they are clear on where their investment will specifically be spent, they can perform a risk and reward evaluation to make a fully informed decision and set goals for your business.

A perfect business budget will prioritise which goals you can achieve in what order, based on realistic measures.

Your budget plan can help you spot your most problematic expenses and costs.

HERE IS an example of accountably setting goals, strategies, measures, and targets in your business budget:

| Goal (What you will try to achieve? | Strategy (How you will achieve it?) | Measures (What are the inputs and outputs?) | Targets (Quantifiable, time-based) |
|---|---|---|---|
| Offer and sell more | Increase marketing and advertising | Amount sold | Conversion of enquiries to sales |
| Generate how many £$ this week/month | Run face-to-face/online sessions | Meet weekly/monthly projected revenue | Number of new sessions booked |
| Offer and fill 2 more sessions | Ask current clients for referrals and social media marketing | 2 new appointments scheduled | Sessions booked and completed |

*Set goals that are achievable*

## The near-perfect business budget

Estimate your monthly fixed costs. Separate your fixed and variable costs. Firstly, focus on your fixed costs; the consistent and recurring expenses that must be paid every month and keep your business running, such as rent for your office, insurance, credit card fees and costs of leasing or paying back for business hardware.

## Budget your fixed costs

It takes two steps to calculate your monthly fixed costs:

- First list all your fixed expenses.
- Second, add them up to get the total fixed costs of your business. You can also divide this with the number of sessions you give to calculate your fixed cost per session.

Knowing your fixed costs informs you of the bare minimum that you need to survive. Make sure you're getting the best deal for each session you offer.

## Budget your variable expenses

These are all the costs that vary and are not bound by days, weeks, months, or years. Your variable expenses might be travel, resources and materials, marketing, and phone calls, as an example.

The variable costs include the materials and labour that go into each session. The more sessions you give, the higher your variable costs will be.

Choose how you want to quantify your services. Is it by the hours you put into your work? or do see each session as an individual, completed project?

What are the relevant costs for each session run? The hours spent on preparation, the expense of resources, the travel, the time, the cost of using a marketing campaign on social media?

When times are tight, variable costs are often the first to cut as they are the easiest to compromise when you're looking to reduce expenses and increase your profit.

## Predict your single costs

Keep single spending or 'sunk costs' in mind and plan them in your budget.

Single or one-time expenses may include purchasing equipment to own rather than rent, such as a laptop, office furniture or the purchase of a domain name.

For unpredictable single costs that throw your budget, you need to rely on your emergency fund, which I discuss later.

HERE IS an example of an Expense Sheet covering the categories of a large and small business.

| Expense spreadsheet | | | | | | |
| --- | --- | --- | --- | --- | --- | --- |

**Business name**

**Date**

| EXPENSE CATEGORY | JAN | FEB | MAR | APR | MAY | JUN |
| --- | --- | --- | --- | --- | --- | --- |
| **Operating expenses** | | | | | | |
| Advertising spend | - | - | - | - | - | - |
| Direct labour costs | - | - | - | - | - | - |
| Direct material costs | - | - | - | - | - | - |
| Freight or shipping charges | - | - | - | - | - | - |
| Healthcare insurance | - | - | - | - | - | - |
| Storage costs | - | - | - | - | - | - |
| Telephone bills | - | - | - | - | - | - |
| Travelling expenses | - | - | - | - | - | - |
| Utility bills | - | - | - | - | - | - |
| **Non-operating expenses** | | | | | | |
| Interest expenses | - | - | - | - | - | - |
| Legal expenses | - | - | - | - | - | - |
| Loss on disposal of assets | - | - | - | - | - | - |
| Obsolete inventory charges | - | - | - | - | - | - |
| **Capital expenses** | | | | | | |
| Buildings | - | - | - | - | - | - |
| Land | - | - | - | - | - | - |
| Machinery | - | - | - | - | - | - |
| Office equipment | - | - | - | - | - | - |
| Vehicle | - | - | - | - | - | - |
| **MONTH TOTAL** | £0.00 | £0.00 | £0.00 | £0.00 | £0.00 | £0.00 |

*Cover all your expenses*

## Project revenues

When your business begins making money, you need to use your current sales activities to forecast future revenue. With a forecast of revenue, you can estimate the sales you'll be making in the next week, month, and year, providing you with targets to aim for within various timeframes. Ultimately, they allow you to see if you are meeting these targets when they are due.

By comparing your actual revenue versus you projected revenue, you inform your future projected revenue forecasts. It helps you maintain cash flow to ensure you're not caught short.

## Tracking profit and loss

Your net profit margin is the money you're left with after deducting your business expenses, interest, and taxes.

Profit earned is not the same as revenue generated. Revenue is your net sales before deducting any costs. If your revenue is high, your business might still be running at a loss.

It's important to put your financial results into a profit and loss (P&L) statement. With all your business costs identified and your revenue recorded, it only takes addition and subtraction to create your P&L statement.

Add up all the earnings of the month and the expenses incurred. Subtract the expenses from your earnings to see whether your business is making a profit or a loss.

A PROFIT and Loss Statement for a large or small business can be set up to follow an outline like this.

**Estimated Profit and Loss**

**Business name**

**Date**

| Profit & Loss Forecast | January | February | March | April |
|---|---|---|---|---|
| Sales | £0.00 | £0.00 | £0.00 | £0.00 |
| **Cost of sales** | | | | |
| Purchases | £0.00 | £0.00 | £0.00 | £0.00 |
| **Gross Profit** | £0.00 | £0.00 | £0.00 | £0.00 |
| **Overheads** | | | | |
| Accounting fees | - | - | - | - |
| Business use of home | - | - | - | - |
| Delivery | - | - | - | - |
| Depreciation | - | - | - | - |
| Hosting | - | - | - | - |
| Mileage in own car | - | - | - | - |
| Office consumables | - | - | - | - |
| Packaging | - | - | - | - |
| Printing, postage & stationary | - | - | - | - |
| Software | - | - | - | - |
| Staff Salaries | - | - | - | - |
| Staff tax | - | - | - | - |
| Telephone & internet | - | - | - | - |
| Travel | - | - | - | - |
| **Total overheads** | £0.00 | £0.00 | £0.00 | £0.00 |

*Profit and Loss Statements reveal all the issues in your business*

## Adjustments

Adjust your accounts for undersights and oversights. Business budgets must change to adapt to changing trends and external, unpredictable events.

You will have periods of high and low customer demand, and you need to account for these highs and lows in your budget. Note these trends as they occur to help better forecast your future cash flow in the following year.

This allows you to save enough money from busy seasons to cover periods of slower sales. It can also help you decide when you need to ramp up your business marketing and advertising and when to ease it down.

Uncontrollable external events can cause chaos to your business, and this is where your emergency fund comes in handy.

## Create an emergency fund

Emergencies happen and we need to prepare as best we can. Illness, sudden repairs, or replacement of business equipment rises in rent, energy and other bills, customers who don't pay, and legal issues can all occur despite your most careful planning.

Create a financial buffer for unforeseen expenses by saving up an emergency fund.

This fund is for emergencies ONLY! Raise enough savings to cover 6 months of business operations, including all expenses. This may vary from a thousand to several thousand, depending on the scale and expenses of your business.

## Review your Budget

Your budget is an active document and must be kept alive by frequent revisits for effective growth. This will help stop you from the temptation of spending money you can't afford to spare. When completing a monthly review of your business budget, compare the revenue you projected in your budget plan, and the actual income of your business. Analyse any shortfalls or high turnovers for unrealistic targets or unpredicted, external difficulties.

Sorting out a business plan that "mostly works" takes effort, but you need the insights to make informed spending decisions. It will help you avoid risky expenses through being objective and putting the business first.

If budgeting is just not your forte, you need to hire a good accountant. You can also consider investing in accounting software such as QuickBooks Online which will help you manage your incomings and outgoings. Accounting software also has the potential to ease your preparation for tax deadlines.

**16**

## MARKETING: BUILDING A REPUTATION

W ord-of-mouth popularity through a good reputation will likely grow your tutoring quickly. However, depending on your situation and location, you might need to consider further techniques for getting your service out there, especially in areas of high competition.

Tutoring can be a lonely and sometimes isolating experience. Many tutors want to feel part of a team. This is where tutoring agencies can help. Tutoring agencies do the marketing for you, take the payment and deal with all kinds of administration issues and regulations. Even registered with one or more agencies, you can still be a free agent, responsible for your own hours. You will remain self-employed. Be mindful that most agencies take an average of 15 to 30% commission from your fees.

Just be aware that effective marketing typically takes up around 70% of your workload, when you do it yourself.

I have outlined the essence of marketing within this chapter. The rest is your persistence and practise.

.   .   .

To target your market, **you must be able to answer the following key marketing questions:**

**Who is my ideal customer?**

As a tutor you are mainly marketing to parents/guardians, the community and local Education Departments or Boroughs. You might also be marketing directly to schools, if they are interested in your service, and have the means to pay.

To answer this question, review the customers who have bought from you in the past, or others in tutoring. Speak with friends or family who have hired tutors in the past.

Look for the specific characteristics that identify a likely customer. Their socio-economic status, their personality type, their profession and pay scale, the needs of their child, etc. Keep your eyes and ears open for customers who match this same profile.

Where do they live? Location often dictates the fees you charge. Spread your thoughts outwards. Tutoring is now an international business since we have the capacity for accessible, online communication software, such as Zoom.

What age bracket **are the parents in?** Are they in their late 20's, their 30's or 40's?

What is their socio-economic background? Most tutoring requests come from middle to upper-middle class families, keen for their children to succeed, who are aware of the competition of the study and working world.

- What do they buy?
- How do they buy?

- What is their lifestyle like?
- Who do they aspire to be, or who do they want their children to become?

### How do I best reach customers matching the above profile?

Track the time that you spend on various sales activities and see which bring in the results. Focus your effort mainly on areas of marketing that bring results and dabble experimentally in other marketing activities to see how effective they are. Try leaflets, social media, Word-of-mouth promotion and personal and local business connections. See what others are successfully doing in your same area and imitate them. You must persevere. Marketing is one area where you never stop trying and trying again. As you build your business, reputation and recommendation is the prime decider for many parents taking on your services.

### How can I best add value to my customer and student's life?

To answer this question, learn more about what the parent/guardian ultimately wants? Is it a placement in the best school by passing an entrance exam? Is it because they want to build their child's confidence? Is it because they want to give their child the experience of a Private Education because their child attends a state school, and they can't afford private fees? Listen to what parents are saying when they contact you and ask them what their ideal tutor will be able to do for them.

### How can I express my value to my customer in 15 words or less?

Create your own value proposition and edit it down to something short and sweet. You must describe something of value to the customer, not a list of your products and services.

**Why am I better than the competition?**

How are your competitors marketing their products? Fine tune your message (value proposition) to emphasize something that you do best and is unique to your approach and that your customers highly value.

To HONE YOUR MARKETING SKILL, **take a deep dive in the following areas:**

**Improve your customer experience**

- Are your customers aware of all the features, products, and services that you offer?
- How can you measure your customer experience?
- How likely would they be to recommend your service to a friend?
- If they had a magic wand, what would your customers change about your service?
- What might make them stop doing business with you?

**Measure your brand impression**

- How do users perceive your services?
- Does their experience match how you want to be seen?
- Does your brand appear trustworthy?
- What do they like and dislike about the way you present your product or service?
- What words would they use to describe you?
- Would they recommend you?

**Compare your tutor image to a competitor**

- How would you convince them to switch to your tutoring?

- If users are already familiar with tutors, which do they prefer?
- What do people like and dislike about your competitor's newest feature or products?
- Who does a better job of explaining the product or offering clearly?
- Why do they prefer one tutor over another?
- What might convince your current customers to switch to your competitors?

## GET a complete understanding of your webpage or social media

- Why do certain pages have high bounce and exit rates?
- What's really causing users to leave your site at those points?
- Why are conversions lower on mobile than desktop or desktop and mobile?
- Why does one webpage a higher average time spent on page?

### Improve your social media marketing

- How are you using feedback you receive on social media to shape your service?
- How can you continue to replicate your best performing content?
- What are your users talking about on social media?
- What type of content performs best on each social channel?
- What types of requests or complaints are coming in?

### Find out if your copy is effective

- Does your customer understand what you're offering when they land on your homepage for the first time?
- Is your language clear and free of jargon?
- Do you speak like your audience speaks?
- Are you catching their attention with clear and simple 'Call to Action's?'

**Learn what users think of your ads**

- What's the mindset of someone who's encountering your ads for the first time?
- What do people notice, like, and dislike about your ads?
- Are your ads helpful, or simply spam?
- What phrases or design elements capture your audience's eye?

**Optimise your email marketing**

- Why are users opening some of your emails more than others?
- Will your customer understand and engage with your next email campaign?
- What would users change about your emails if they could?
- Do your users receive emails from other companies in your industry?
- Which companies?
- What do they like and dislike about your emails?

**Build higher-converting landing pages**

- Can your target customer understand what's being offered?
- Does it meet, or exceed their expectations for this type of service?
- Do they become distracted by anything?

- Can they easily sign up for it using the forms you've provided?
- Do they think your offer has value, and are they willing to pay money or enter their contact information in exchange for it?
- Is there any other information they would need to see before clicking on a Call to Action?

**Optimise your online forms**

- Do you have too few or too many fields on your form for its purpose?
- Are all your forms accessible to people who use a keyboard or button input device rather than a mouse?
- Do the forms work correctly and smoothly on all devices and all screen sizes?
- If a user makes a mistake when filling out a form, do your error messages help them correct the mistake right away?
- Is there anything about your form that would make a user give up?

**How do users discover your services through organic search?**

- What comes up when users search for keywords related to your site: your website, your competitors, etc.
- What words stand out to them on the Google search results page?
- When they click on your link, what do they expect to find?
- Does your landing page meet those expectations?

## Content Marketing Explained

Content on social media may seem easy to create; however, it is often difficult to convert a visitor into a customer. An Instagram story may last only seconds; however, it has typically taken many minutes or hours to produce. Every single piece of branded content you encounter was designed as part of a content marketing strategy to turn you from a visitor to a lead.

Social media is complex, and you must continually try new approaches to capture attention, while not misrepresenting your service. People are constantly flicking through the constant flow of new content that appears before their eyes every second. How will you stand out to that parent/guardian in a brief moment, who has tutoring in mind for their child?

## You need content marketing

You are trying to generate traffic and leads. Content marketing influences the customer's buying decision. It offers useful information to build trust with potential customers. From that trust, a relationship is established and nurtured with further content, and hopefully, personal contact.

Content marketing isn't designed to sell, which is why it differs from advertising. Content marketing provides answers questions, and provides solutions to problems, or simply entertains and distracts. By providing your expertise and insight by answering these questions, your business becomes a source of trusted information. Your business can use content marketing to increase interest in your services and build long-term relationships.

## Improve your content marketing

- Do users find your information and presentation helpful and relevant?

- When a user views your content, what do they want to know?
- What part of your content catches their eye first?
- Do your competitors offer better content?
- What content would your customer like to see you present next?

## You need a strategy for your website

Designing a strategy ensures you focus your time and resources on creating the right content, reaching the right audience, and increasing traffic to your business. By carefully selecting the content and topics you create, you'll attract people more likely to purchase your services.

## Scrutinise

Scrutinising will identify what content performs well, and where to improve.

What do you want your content to achieve for your business?

According to the Content Marketing Institute, 79% of content marketers are focused on building brand awareness first and foremost to create future sales.

HERE ARE some probing ways to make use of Google Analytics (https://support.google.com/analytics/answer/1008015?hl=en) to find out what content on your website works for your audience, and what doesn't:

- Find out your popularity and number of visits
- Find out your bounce rate on your site. Your bounce rate is the percentage of visitors who navigate away from your site after viewing only one page.

- Find out the demographics of your Audience and their location

To MANUALLY TRACK **your audience's awareness of you in social media, monitor the following:**

- Your Brand awareness amongst your audience by impressions, mentions, shares, likes and links to your content.
- Your audience growth rate, i.e., how many new followers you have after every 3 months.
- Your follower growth across your channels.
- Your new Sign-up's to email-capture lists.

**Additionally:**

- Scrutinise what your competitors do differently to you.
- Scrutinise the topics are most popular in their content.

**You Need to Provide solutions**

- It's crucial to step into your customer's shoes.
- What do they care about?
- What matters most to them? For example, is it convenience?
- How can they make their life easier with the aid of your service?

Great content solves your audience's problems.

- Put yourself in the shoes of your best customer.
- What are they thinking about?

- What challenges do they face?

Write down at least 3 things they possibly have on their mind. For each of these 3 topics, think about how your business can provide solutions. Write down 3 ways forward for every challenge. 3 challenges multiplied by 3 solutions will help you produce 9 content ideas to create.

## Produce Better Content

Consider using video as it is the most engaging format across all social media. YouTube is still the primary social media channel for users aged 18 to 64. TikTok is more popular with teens to 25-year-olds, and Instagram and Facebook are used more by those in their 20's to 60's.

- Do you have the skills and resources to create good copy and content?
- Consider the length of time it will take from creation to production.
- Who will be doing your SEO (Search Engine Optimization)?
- Who will be editing and fact-checking your content?
- What time will you publish? It's essential that you post at the right time, so schedule carefully to get the most views.

## The Best times to post on social media as of 2021

### Twitter:

**Best times:** Wednesday 9 a.m.– 3 p.m., Tuesday through Thursday 9–11 a.m.

**Best day:** Wednesday
**Worst day:** Saturday

**Instagram:**

**Best times:** Tuesday, Wednesday, and Friday 9 a.m.–1 p.m.
  **Best days:** Tuesday, Wednesday, Friday
  **Worst day:** Saturday


**LinkedIn:**

**Best times:** Tuesday through Thursday 9 a.m.–noon
  **Best days:** Tuesday and Wednesday
  **Worst day:** Sunday


**Facebook:**

**Best times:** Tuesday, Wednesday, and Friday 9 a.m.–1 p.m.
  **Best days:** Tuesday, Wednesday, Friday
  **Worst day:** Saturday


**Blog:**

Friday at noon.
  Sprout Social 2021 (https://sproutsocial.com/insights/best-times-to-post-on-social-media/)


Social Media, and Google Advertising and Analytics are constantly changing and take much scrutiny to manage. You can see why marketing through this medium will take up so much of your time. Your best bet for initial marketing is to begin in your local area, making a personal connection with people in your community to build awareness, reputation and hopefully their recommendation to others for your great service.

17

# SETTING A PRICE AND DEALING WITH OBJECTIONS

There are a variety of factors to take into consideration when determining your price. In this brief chapter I outline common-sense pricing and why you should be pricing in the way that you do. You should not have to spend hours deciding on your price. Your price should be simple and clear-cut.

When you first start tutoring, begin with one model of pricing and only after you build your practice, consider offering further pricing choices.

**Consider Your Time**

Your personal preparation and revision

The age group you are tutoring and therefore the length of time

Whether you are tutoring face-to-face or online

Whether you offer 30 minutes, 45 minutes or 1-hour sessions

The time you need transitioning between lessons before your next session. Time is typically lost in-between sessions.

How long you travel to and from the tutoring session.

## Consider your Expenses

Resource costs
  Travel costs
  Home costs
  Cancelled lesson costs and how much notice you require and what charge for a last-minute cancellation.
  Tax


## Consider your Customer's Location

If you are tutoring in an affluent area, you can charge the going rate for tutoring in the area. However, just because parents may have a good income, doesn't mean that they won't drive a hard bargain.

In less affluent areas, you should price fairly to meet the income of the parent. All parents want their children to do well at school and ensure they have a good future. As educators we want to give what we can to help this happen. Consider teaching small groups of students where parents with low incomes can pool their money to afford your service.

The International market can be quite lucrative for the tutoring service you provide. There are many affluent parents out there in big cities seeking a UK or USA education for their child. Marketing is a little more difficult if you are trying to enter the foreign tutoring market and you will likely find yourself reliant on established international tutoring agencies at the sacrifice of a percentage of your income.


## Your Personal Capability, Reputation, Experience and Qualifications

- Do you get the results you promise?
- Do you get the results in a timely way?
- What do you do exactly to improve the student

academically and in terms of their subject and personal confidence?

- Do you teach the student how to organise themselves and study?
- Do you provide valuable follow-up homework and support?
- Do your students enjoy your tutoring?
- After reading these factors, at this point, what figure do you have in mind so far?
- Are you thinking too much about the needs of your customer and assuming what they can afford?

Read on to further refine what you should be charging.

## Handling Parent objections

Parents typically don't understand teaching and tutoring as a profession. Here are the two most likely objections to your service and why you should not cave in under pressure:

"Your price is too high!": They may think you are only worth $20/£20. This is a typical assumption as many mass-volume tutoring agencies offer cheap tutoring from tutors living in less-affluent countries where £20/$20 goes a much longer way in life. So, it's true, they can get a cheaper service if they like. They can even hire a local High School student for far less than a professional tutor. The difference in your specific experience, planning, knowledge, delivery and post-session quality homework is where your price-point is justified.

You must have faith in your experience and reputation. Don't even compromise unless you really think it will benefit you. Hold out on your desperation for work. If you start charging less, word will get around that you charge less and you will be working extremely hard to scrape together a living.

## Handling Price

You need to outline your pricing in an attractive way: highlight the planning, knowledge, gifts you bring, plus the follow-up homework and your support. It needs to sound like a guarantee that you will deliver a great experience and improve their child's life. Do not make promises about particular levels or grades that their child will achieve.

Remember, that if you were working in a school, what would you be paid? In a tutoring session, you are offering more pure education value than in a school as you are focusing on one person to a small group, and not a whole class.

See your role as distilling strategies and methods into convenient "gifts of learning." As you have little time to get your points across, you have to get to the heart of your subject while enriching and exciting your students with the experiences you deliver.

"Zoom/Online lessons should be cheap!": Many parents will argue that because the session is on Zoom, it's not as good. Well, my experience of teaching on Zoom has always proven to be an effective way of teaching. Focus is just as strong, and you get through the same amount of material. You also complete the same amount of planning, prepare resources, and set homework, as you would face-to-face.

Ensure that you set yourself up for high quality online teaching and market this to your potential clients. Light yourself properly, use a quality webcam, and if the sound is not good, a quality microphone. Separate yourself from your background using a lamp lighting your backdrop or wall. Create a backdrop set that reflects learning and knowledge. Have appropriate books on a bookshop, or a motivational poster about learning. You need to create a professional image. Walk the parent through how you teach and what you provide for further learning and support.

Know that someone will pay you what you are worth, as long as you are not being delusional about your own value, with prices that would make anyone step back with draw-dropping shock.

Having worked in London in the UK, the average range of prices varies between professional tutors from £30 to £80. I have heard of much higher prices, and I have also heard of those charging lower, usually students making a little pocket money. If you are in an agency being paid £40, don't be surprised to find that the parent may be paying your agency up to £20 more, which the agency is snaffling as commission.

Primary tutoring will likely earn less than those who are teaching upper GCSE and A Level. However, primary tutors who are preparing students for 11+ entrance examination will likely charge more as there is an intensity to the work and deadlines to meet.

**If you want to ease parent objections:**

- Be friendly and understanding
- Be approachable and willing to give that little bit more
- Be professional in your feedback
- Be forthcoming about your talents and what you have achieved when tutoring other students
- Draw upon your local reputation as a tutor
- Guarantee progress for a student in a way that the parent/guardian can understand, and then go out of your way for it to happen.

Your ultimate aim is for your reputation to grow, and word-of-mouth to do most of the marketing work for you, so you can concentrate on quality teaching.

PART I

---

# APPENDICES OF TUTORING RESOURCES

18

# RECOMMENDED TUTORING RESOURCES

It can be difficult starting as a tutor as costs can be high. However, you will need to invest in resources at some point, and I recommend the following as you begin to build.

School revision guides for your subject/s and Year groups save you a lot of time in knowing what to teach. They range from State and Private targeted revision. It will help you cut through the swathes of teaching materials to prep a student appropriately for their targeted tests. You can find many revision guides in second-hand bookshops and charity stores as parents tend to buy them for their children and then end up donating them, often with them receiving no use at all. Parents often do not have the skill, or the will, to self-teach or monitor their own children in their education.

Sample tests are freely available on the internet for you to research and follow with your student preparation. They range from UK SATs and 11+ to US SAT. You can even find the tests that have been used in certain schools. So, if your student is aiming for admission in St Swithin's School for the Gifted and Talented (made-up name), you will likely find an entrance examination for English and Maths online somewhere. Don't forget non-verbal reasoning tests are a common practice in selective schools and just take exposure and practise for most students to improve performance.

For worksheets, lesson plans, curriculum maps and other great resources, I recommend a membership to a top educational resource online provider, such as Twinkl.com. You can also register for free at TES.com (Times Educational Supplement) for online resources and pay for resources that others have created. There are dozens of resource sites out there and you need to choose what covers the curriculums you are teaching in the borough, county, or state you are teaching in. You want clear, practical, and uncomplicated worksheets to complement your teaching and provide you with a quick resource for homework. You'll be surprised how much you must prepare for a successful tutoring session.

IF YOU WISH to assign tasks from any subject area and monitor the progress of your student, join senecalearning.com. It's a fantastic programme that allows anyone around the world, including those living in impoverished conditions to access learning (only if they can access the internet.) The range of subjects and specific curriculums and modules is excellent. If you pay for membership, you will receive extra materials, resources, and capabilities for better tracking your students. If you are beginning and struggling, you can join for free. If you are a teacher or tutor not attached to a school, you can register as a parent and then change this after to "teacher" in settings.

**HERE ARE some other resources that are worthwhile for improving your practice:**

- Stickers, certificates, and small rewards such as stationary, for your younger students.
- If you have a laptop, raise it to eye level using large books or any other riser. This means you will need an additional keyboard and mouse.

- Drawing tablet and pen, such as a Wacom. You can also look into hooking up your interactive tablet (iPad, Android, Windows) to draw directly to the Zoom whiteboard.
- A separate condenser microphone, such as a Blue Yeti with a USB connection for the richest and clearest sound than the tinny sound that built in microphones often produce.
- A ring light is perfect for soft, even face lighting, and they are relatively cheap to buy.
- Light the wall behind you with a any lamp pointed at it to separate you from your background.
- Zoom account. A free account for one-to-one tutoring. You will need a paid account for small groups running beyond 40 minutes, and for Webinars you intend to reach over 100 people for.
- Use your Smart phone. Take photos of your students work and post it on social media. Ensure you don't post any personal details of the child or any backgrounds that can identify them, including just the first name. **<u>DO NOT</u>** photograph a child, ever! The rule is to photograph work only, with their parent/guardian's permission. I cannot emphasise this enough. In the UK you would be breaching Safeguarding and Child Protection legislation, and possibly putting that student in danger.
- If you need to use photographs of children learning in your marketing, use photographs online from reputable photo stock sales sites such as Shutterstock. Do not use photographs that you search for on Google images as they likely come with a copyright that you need to pay for.
- If you intend to create digital courses, you can use any video editor. I have used Final Cut Pro and Camtasia; however, there are many free editors available: Audacity is great for recording audio. Apple iMovie, Lightworks and Hitfilm Express are some great movie editors. You can

even just record a mock lesson through Zoom using its record function.

- Accounting software such as Quickbooks online will help you create and send invoices and receipts and prepare your quarterly or yearly tax. You can upload your receipts and connect your banking account/s for ease of financial management. If you do not understand tax yet, invest in a course and/or hire a tax accountant for your first year.

# 19

# 99 ENGAGING IDEAS FOR TUTORING IN-PERSON AND ONLINE

- 1. Boggle. Shake a box full of alphabet letter dice or use any other way to generate random letters. Make as many words as you can from the resulting letters.
- 2. Build a Story. Start with a few words and ask your student to add three more. Keep alternating until you have a paragraph or two and then ask them to read it out. Model good writing.
- 3. Build a vehicle that can transport a small object from one side of the room to the other.
- 4. Bulls and Cows. One player thinks up a secret word of a set number of letters. The second player guesses a word; the first player tells them how many letters match in the right position (bulls) and how many letters are correct but in the wrong position (cows).
- 5. Choose a famous person and write a fictional historical diary from their point of view.
- 6. Choose a multiplication table and teach them the patterns within it and strategies to learn. There are plenty of finger methods to solve times-tables, including the trickiest, 6 to 9 multiplication tables.

- 7. Choose characters from different books and combine them in a new story, where the traits of their character determine the storyline.
- 8. Compose questions for them to ask in an interview with a family member. What would they like to ask and find out about them? Interview them as homework.
- 9. Compose questions to ask family members about their own life and memories of the past.
- 10. Consequences. This is a fun way to generate a random story. Each player writes down one line of a story and folds the paper over before passing it to the next player or their partner. You can put constraints on it, such as: First line: introduce character, Second line: description of setting, Third line: character speaks, Fourth line: create an atmosphere, Fifth line: something happens. Once complete, the student opens up the paper and reads it out.
- 11. Create a 'still life' picture of a bowl of fruit, or a collection of objects to hand.
- 12. Create a 'treasure map' to help somebody else find something you have hidden.
- 13. Create a biological profile on a living creature and expand it into its habitat and surrounding resources. Create a food chain too.
- 14. Create a comic strip of a sequence of events, timelines or processes.
- 15. Create a composition using an art programme on their laptop/tablet.
- 16. Create a maths test to explain and then give to a member of your family. Include the answers hidden on the back of the sheet.
- 17. Create a partner story. You write one sentence; they write the next. This is your chance to model extended sentence writing.
- 18. Create a persuasive advert to encourage people to buy it using "sales" language.

- 19. Create a portrait of a pet or family member.
- 20. Create a quiz about your favourite topic and test other people's knowledge.
- 21. Create a record of the weather for each day, including temperature inside and outside and humidity.
- 22. Create a scavenger Hunt. Come up with an idea for an object related to the topic being taught and the student should go find and then run back to the screen to share it.
- 23. Create a shop with labels and prices, using surrounding objects and play buying and selling and practise giving change.
- 24. Create a simple animation or gif that tells a story. Use Apple Keynote slides or Powerpoint to design each scene and then save as a gif.
- 25. Create a simple online exercise routine to break up study.
- 26. Create a timeline showing the main events in your life so far.
- 27. Crosswords. Your student either completes a topic related crossword or creates one using the numerous crossword-designing tools free on the internet.
- 28. Design a book cover for a book you are reading.
- 29. Design a healthy meal and an unhealthy meal.
- 30. Design a home for a book character that suits their personality, era and class.
- 31. Design a superhero and show their superpowers through drawing and labelling.
- 32. Design and make your own card game to help remember facts on a topic.
- 33. Design clothes for a toy that suit a purpose, such as being waterproof.
- 34. Do a shape search. Where can you find a parallelogram, semicircle in an everyday object?
- 35. Draw a bird's eye view of a building or area.

- 36. Draw a map showing a known route and its features along the way.
- 37. Draw a new illustration for a part of a story reflecting the mood and the action taking place.
- 38. Draw a picture from a random squiggle on a page, turning it into a recognisable object.
- 39. Draw a picture without lifting your pencil from the page.
- 40. Draw a poster that shows all of the people and things that make you smile.
- 41. Draw a self-portrait using a mirror or laptop/tablet camera.
- 42. Draw It. Dedicate a part of your session to communicating concepts through drawing only. All questions and answers must be drawn.
- 43. Draw or paint a landscape picture of their surroundings or outside their window.
- 44. Explore gases, liquids and solids using ice.
- 45. Hangman. One player thinks of a word from their spellings or a key word from the topic being studied and writes down dashes to represent the number of letters. The other guesses the word by working through probable letters in the alphabet. Correct letters are inserted into the word; incorrect letters result in another segment of the "hangman" being drawn.
- 46. Invent a machine or other technology that solves a problem.
- 47. Investigate floating and sinking in a bowl of water away from any electronic equipment.
- 48. Learn the dance moves for different songs and then perform them.
- 49. Look at a bus, train or plane timetable to practise time problems.
- 50. Make a board game that uses numbers, sums and penalties when you land on certain points.

- 51. Make a factual poster about a period in History such as the Ancient Mayans.
- 52. Make a map of your bedroom, showing where everything is located.
- 53. Make a rainfall measure(raingauge) and chart to record the amount of daily rainfall.
- 54. Make an environmental poster that reflects the cause of damage and what can be done to reduce the damage caused by humanity.
- 55. Make shadow puppets to perform a story.
- 56. Measure challenge. Ask your student to find three objects near them that equal approximately a metre and then line them up and measure them with a ruler or tape measure. Vary the measurement and the number of objects for a challenge.
- 57. Measure objects around the house and then order them according to their size, volume etc?
- 58. Play 'I Spy' to practise phonic sounds.
- 59. Play 'Pictionary'. Draw a picture that represents a favourite book or film without using words and ask someone else to guess what it is.
- 60. Play "Would you rather?" Give each player a choice of two options. They have to choose one and say why. The ideas can be serious or silly but must relate to the topic of study.
- 61. Play Charades related to the topic being taught.
- 62. Play Connect 4 to practise strategy and practising staying one step ahead of your partner.
- 63. Play noughts and crosses/tic-tac-toe for strategy and plotting ahead.
- 64. Play the alphabet game. Choose a category and go through the alphabet, thinking of an example that begins with every letter.
- 65. Play the squares game where you take turns adding one side to a grid with the purpose of completing a square

which you then initial. You attempt to prevent your partner completing a square. Each square you make, gives you an extra turn.

- 66. Play the yes/no game. Take it in turns to ask each other questions. The person being asked is out if they answer "yes" or "no". How creative can you make your answers?
- 67. Reporter. Ask you student to interview you as a historic or fictional character. They have to take notes on your factual attempts at answers and then compose it as a report.
- 68. Scattergories. Choose a letter and a list of categories related to your topic, such as characters, atmosphere, scenes, events, etc, and tell your student to come up with as many answers as possible. Give them a couple of minutes per round.
- 69. Search the products in their house for where they were manufactures and how far they have travelled and the distance in miles or kilometres.
- 70. Some Preparation
- 71. Start a number pattern and continue it as long as possible. Try primes, square numbers, cubes, or work backwards from larger numbers, halving, quartering or squaring.
- 72. Story Cubes. Use story cubes (large dice) to create a random structure for a story. My favourite is to use a series of sentence starts that must be written in the order they are rolled, e.g. adverb, speech, description, atmosphere, new scene, performing an action, etc.
- 73. Teach the teacher. Ask the pupil to present how to solve a sum or problem, compose and essay or sentence, or teach an area they have researched to you. They can use a slideshow or a series of drawings, or whatever creative way they can imaging to get their points across.
- 74. Theme Day. Pick a theme for a session related to the

topic being studied, such as wear a hat, change your hairstyle, wear a costume, to get into the mood of study.

- 75. Think of some jokes to memorise and tell.
- 76. Try yoga exercises, mindfulness and breathing activities.
- 77. Tweet Facts. Give your student a limit the length of a Tweet (140 characters), to describe a fact from the topic they are studying.
- 78. Two Truths and a Lie with a Twist. Ask students to pretend to be a famous character and create statements in regard to what they are studying. Your student comes up with two statements or facts that are true and one that is not. They share it to see if you can figure it out. You can do the same for them.
- 79. Use a virtual reality headset and google to visit places around the world relevant to the settings of their study.
- 80. Use materials to make a model of a famous building from an era being studied.
- 81. Use paper to make a bridge that spans a gap and can carry a toy car.
- 82. Virtual background. On Zoom or another online platform, change your virtual background to fit the theme of study, such as Dicken's Victorian London.
- 83. What does this object do? Put together a number of objects from the past, related to the topic being studied, in a series of pictures, and see if they can work out their function or purpose.
- 84. What hopes and dreams do you have for the future? Draw a picture to show what you hope life will be like in 10, 20 or even 50 years!
- 85. What's the question? Give your student an answer and ask them for three questions that lead to the specific answer.
- 86. Where am I? Change your virtual background to a

location and see if they can guess where you are. Ask them to change their background too.

- 87. Who Said It? Write a series of quotes from a text and see how many your student can match to the characters who said them.
- 88. Word searches. Your student either solves a word search using topic keywords or creates one using a free online wordsearch creator.
- 89. Write "Top 10" lists of book characters, story highlights, or any interesting topic, ranking them in order.
- 90. Write a book review of a book they are reading and comment on the strengths and weaknesses of the storyline and features.
- 91. Write a dictionary to record any new keywords and their meaning, in alphabetical order.
- 92. Write a letter to a friend or family member. What would they like to tell them about?
- 93. Write a letter to their favourite author.
- 94. Write a news report about something newsworthy that has occurred recently.
- 95. Write a set of instructions to teach people how to play a simple game or sport.
- 96. Write an alternative ending to a story.
- 97. Write an exciting blurb to sell a story you are reading.
- 98. Write thank you notes to people you appreciate and leave them around the house.
- 99. Write up a menu for lunch, dinner, or a fantasy dinner for a famous person or character from a story they are studying.

**20**

---

# PLANNING AND BUDGET SHEETS

# Fast Planning Sheet

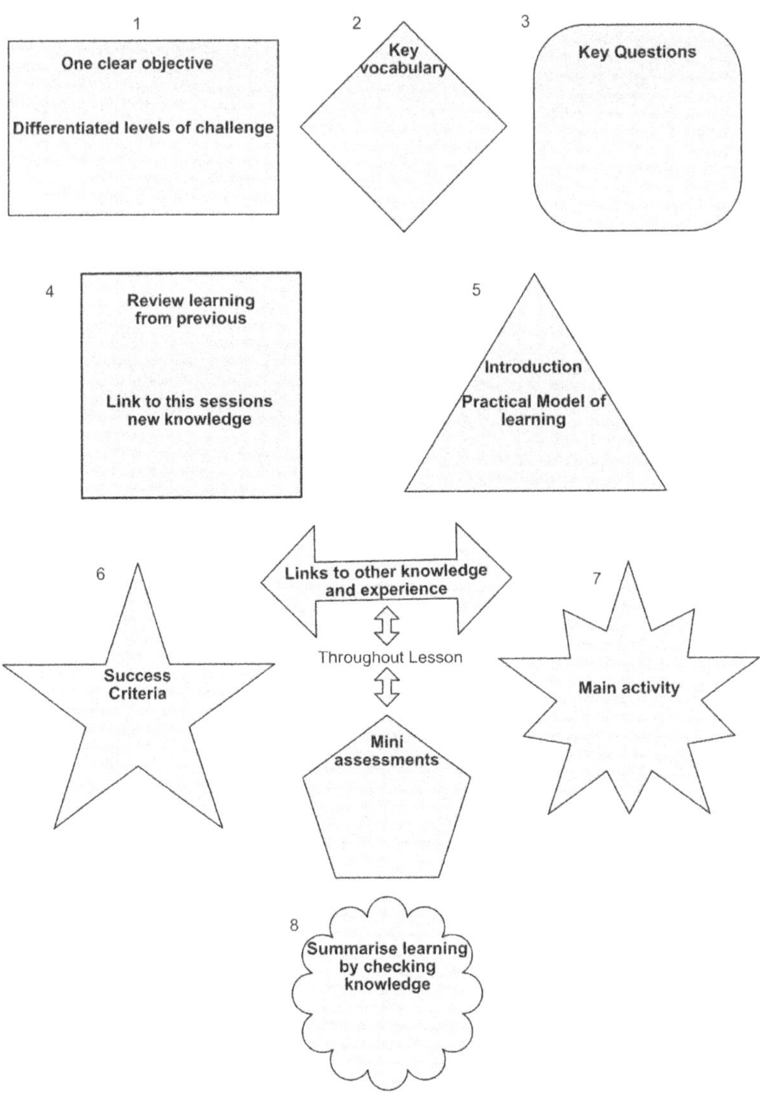


*How to rapidly plan a lesson*

## Full Lesson Plan

| Lesson: | | Year Group: | Date: |
|---|---|---|---|
| Prior Knowledge, Skills and Understanding: | | Ability: | Duration: |
| | | Activity: | |

Learning Intentions/Learning Objective:

| Key Session Points | Points to Remember: Key Learning & Teaching Strategies |
|---|---|
| Introduction:<br>• | Resources:<br><br>Key Vocabulary: |
| Activities and Experiences:<br>• | Key Questions: |
| Conclusion/ Plenary:<br>• | Differentiation: |
| Cross Curricular Links: | |
| Success Criteria:<br>•<br>•<br>• | Assessment Methods: |
| Evaluation/ Next Steps: | |

*A full plan covering all the important areas of learning*

## Startup Costs

**Your company name**

**Date**

| Item Cost | # of Months | Monthly Cost | Total Cost |
|---|---|---|---|
| **MONTHLY COSTS** | | | |
| Accounting Fees | | | |
| Employee Payroll Taxes and Benefits | | | £0.00 |
| Employee Salaries | | | £0.00 |
| Insurance | | | £0.00 |
| Interest | | | £0.00 |
| Legal Fees | | | £0.00 |
| Ongoing Advertising/Promotion | | | £0.00 |
| Rent/Lease Payments | | | £0.00 |
| Staff Salaries | | | £0.00 |
| Subcriptions | | | £0.00 |
| Supplies | | | £0.00 |
| Utilities | | | £0.00 |
| Miscellaneous | | | £0.00 |
| **TOTAL MONTHLY COSTS** | | | **£0.00** |
| **SINGLE COSTS** | | | |
| Advertising/Promotion | | | £0.00 |
| Business Licenses/Permits/Fees | | | £0.00 |
| Business Registration | | | £0.00 |
| Cash-On-Hand (Working Capital) | | | £0.00 |
| Consultant(s) | | | £0.00 |
| Furniture | | | £0.00 |
| Inventory | | | £0.00 |
| Machinery and Equipment | | | £0.00 |
| Software | | | £0.00 |
| Website Design & Development | | | £0.00 |
| Miscellaneous | | | £0.00 |
| **TOTAL ONE-TIME COSTS** | | | **£0.00** |
| **TOTAL STARTUP COSTS** | | | **£0.00** |

*Startup*

## Expense spreadsheet

**Business name**

**Date**

| EXPENSE CATEGORY | JAN | FEB | MAR | APR | MAY | JUN |
|---|---|---|---|---|---|---|
| **Operating expenses** | | | | | | |
| Advertising spend | - | - | - | - | - | - |
| Direct labour costs | - | - | - | - | - | - |
| Direct material costs | - | - | - | - | - | - |
| Freight or shipping charges | - | - | - | - | - | - |
| Healthcare insurance | - | - | - | - | - | - |
| Storage costs | - | - | - | - | - | - |
| Telephone bills | - | - | - | - | - | - |
| Travelling expenses | - | - | - | - | - | - |
| Utility bills | - | - | - | - | - | - |
| **Non-operating expenses** | | | | | | |
| Interest expenses | - | - | - | - | - | - |
| Legal expenses | - | - | - | - | - | - |
| Loss on disposal of assets | - | - | - | - | - | - |
| Obsolete inventory charges | - | - | - | - | - | - |
| **Capital expenses** | | | | | | |
| Buildings | - | - | - | - | - | - |
| Land | - | - | - | - | - | - |
| Machinery | - | - | - | - | - | - |
| Office equipment | - | - | - | - | - | - |
| Vehicle | - | - | - | - | - | - |
| **MONTH TOTAL** | £0.00 | £0.00 | £0.00 | £0.00 | £0.00 | £0.00 |

*Expenses*

## Estimated Profit and Loss

**Business name**

Date

| Profit & Loss Forecast | January | February | March | April |
|---|---|---|---|---|
| Sales | £0.00 | £0.00 | £0.00 | £0.00 |
| **Cost of sales** | | | | |
| Purchases | £0.00 | £0.00 | £0.00 | £0.00 |
| **Gross Profit** | £0.00 | £0.00 | £0.00 | £0.00 |
| **Overheads** | | | | |
| Accounting fees | - | - | - | - |
| Business use of home | - | - | - | - |
| Delivery | - | - | - | - |
| Depreciation | - | - | - | - |
| Hosting | - | - | - | - |
| Mileage in own car | - | - | - | - |
| Office consumables | - | - | - | - |
| Packaging | - | - | - | - |
| Printing, postage & stationary | - | - | - | - |
| Software | - | - | - | - |
| Staff Salaries | - | - | - | - |
| Staff tax | - | - | - | - |
| Telephone & internet | - | - | - | - |
| Travel | - | - | - | - |
| **Total overheads** | £0.00 | £0.00 | £0.00 | £0.00 |

*Profit and Loss*

| Goal (What you will try to achieve? | Strategy (How you will achieve it?) | Measures (What are the inputs and outputs?) | Targets (Quantifiable, time-based) |
|---|---|---|---|
| Offer and sell more ___ | Increase marketing and advertising | Amount sold | Conversion of enquiries to sales |
| Generate how many £$ this week/month | Run face-to-face/online sessions | Meet weekly/monthly projected revenue | Number of new sessions booked |
| Offer and fill 2 more sessions | Ask current clients for referrals and social media marketing | 2 new appointments scheduled | Sessions booked and completed |

*Budgeting goals*

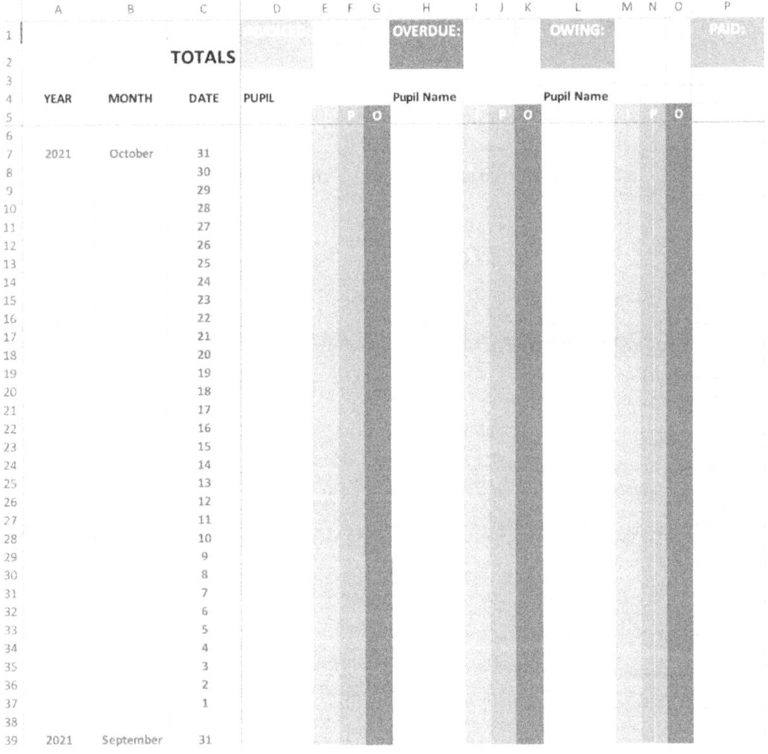


*Know when your clients have been invoiced, have paid or are yet to pay*

# 21

# GETTING YOUR BUSINESS TERMS AND CONDITIONS RIGHT

My advice is to have all your contracts drawn up by an expert in your countries law.

However, here follows advice on the purpose and content of a Terms and Conditions document.

YOUR TERMS and conditions document is the contract between you and your customer for your supply of goods or services. You offer your services on a "take-it-or-leave-it" basis.

## Why use terms and conditions?

Terms and conditions record what you have agreed and present the constrained terms under which you'll accept business:

- Defining the contract
- Setting out business procedures
- Protecting your business and your rights
- Limiting your liability

IT's EASIER to have good Terms and Conditions in place to help avoid legal action, than to defend an unclear contract later.

## Contents of a T&C document

A good terms and conditions document should include:

- Definition of the subject matter of the contract
- Terms that make clear what you are selling.
- The services are described in detail or by reference to another document, such as your sales brochure or web site.

IT's valid to use general words, such as "services set out in our web site" or "the products listed in our catalogue", if your terms cover various situations.

## The price

Include all variations and circumstances as well as provisions for increase.

As price may vary, it is good practice to put it in a separate schedule or refer to it as in "my/our price list from time to time". Set out conditions under which you may change the price, how you will tell your client about the change and whether it will affect this contract.

Set out the circumstances of the increase and how the client needs to give notice if they wish to terminate if they don't accept the new price.

. . .

THE METHOD and timing of payment that's acceptable to you

Your contract should include late payment provisions. This should include default and penalty provisions.

AVOID sales talk such as "We will endeavour to provide a 24 hour service". The purpose of the document is to enhance and protect your interest, not promote your business or protect your customer.

## What happens while the contract runs?

Important in a sale of service, as a consultant or tutor. These provisions would include reporting, testing, staff to be used and any number of other practical points required to deliver your service.

## Termination provisions

## You need to consider:

- How long will your contract last?
- What will trigger the termination?
- What will happen to services not yet delivered?
- What penalties will you seek for early termination?
- How will you prove your losses?
- If you are creating a "product" like software, to whom will it belong if the contract is terminated early?
- Is this clear in your sales material and web site?

## Limitation of your liability

These terms limit the damages that you have to pay to your customer if your goods or services fail. They cover situations such as:

- What happens if you don't provide the goods or services as advertised?

- What if the goods are defective?
- What defect constitutes a reason for the goods to be returned?
- What if your services are inadequate and how is "inadequate" defined?

## Protecting your business from your client

This includes a confidentiality clause, provisions about ownership of intellectual property and unexpected action by a third party.

Use and ownership of intellectual property is particularly important in the context of an internet business.

## Indemnity by your client

An indemnity is a statement that sets out the circumstances in which your client may be liable to re-pay you for your losses and expenses.

## Data protection and privacy

You must tell clients how you intend to comply, by telling them what data you hold and why.

If you have a website, refer to your privacy notice as displayed on your website.

## Dispute resolution

Of course it is sensible to set out in advance how you intend to resolve a problem between you. You want a process to mediate a dispute before any costly and time-consuming legal actions and processes are triggered.

## Statutory rights and consumer protection

Where law made by Parliament sets out the rights of the other party, you cannot reduce those rights in your contract. For example, if under consumer contracts law, a customer has a right to send an item back to you for a full refund within 2 weeks of purchase, you cannot reduce this period to 7 days. You can, however, extend your customers' rights, for example, to 4 weeks.

In English law, consumers enjoy extensive protection not given to a business. If you fail to provide this, not only are you at risk of being closed down by your local trading standards officer, but you may be subject to legal action by your buyer in respect of which your T&C may be no defence.

Imagine you are the buyer, should you accept the contract put to you by the seller?

## Specifically for a website and online practice

If you run a blog, a reference website, an online magazine or newspaper or a community site, your terms should cover ownership of content and rules regulating visitor behaviour.

## Terms for sites that connect buyers and sellers

Sites that connect buyers and sellers are marketplace websites. The market may be for goods or services and may require either side to register as a member before being allowed to trade. These terms include rules for transactions to which your site is not party, and behaviour as a registered buyer or seller.

## Terms for sites that require membership or subscription

Websites that foster a community, whether online or offline, require additional terms relating to behaviour as part of that community.

## Website terms and conditions

Your website terms and conditions form the contract between you and your site visitor, and if you sell online, your customers. Without that contract, it is much harder to protect your business if your site visitors behave in a way that is detrimental to it. Without good website terms and conditions, you may forfeit your rights in law, or you may break the law and become liable for significant fines.

HAVING strong security terms in a website terms and conditions document is not going to stop crime, but it does:

- Provide a deterrent to any misuse for which you could sue in court
- Prevent you being blamed for a criminal activity
- Reduce the chance of you being targeted in a negative social medium campaign
- Assist in protecting you from what someone else posts to your website
- Provide permission for you to remove offensive content and stay in full control of what happens on your website

## Basis of a contract

You cannot impose rules. You can only make a contract.

A contract is only formed if your visitor ticks a box to do so explicitly, or electronically signs a form.

# USEFUL SITES AND LINKS

Www.revisionworld.co.uk
http://senecalearning.com/
www.bbc.co.uk/learning
www.deni.gov.uk
www.education.gov.uk
www.ltscotland.org.uk
www.sqa.org.uk
www.wales.gov.uk
http://www.tes.co.uk

# CONTACT

Thank you for reading this book. If you would like help training as a tutor, please visit my website: miniteaching.com

Contact me at hello@miniteaching.com with any questions you would like answered. Wishing you all the best with your tutoring business,

Andrew-John Paterson

Made in the USA
Coppell, TX
07 August 2024

35701153R00095